Grade 3

Scott Foresman

Leveled Reader

Teaching Guide

PEARSON
Scott Foresman

Editorial Offices: Glenview, Illinois • Parsippany, New Jersey • New York, New York
Sales Offices: Boston, Massachusetts • Duluth, Georgia • Glenview, Illinois
Coppell, Texas • Sacramento, California • Mesa, Arizona

ISBN: 0-328-16909-9

4 5 6 7 8 9 10 V084 12 11 10 09 08 07 06

Table of Contents

LEVELED READER TITLE	Instruction	Comprehension Practice	Vocabulary Practice
The California Gold Rush: A Letter Home	12–13	14	15
It's a Fair Swap!	16–17	18	19
Making Sense of Dollars and Cents	20–21	22	23
Davis Buys a Dog	24–25	26	27
E-Pals	28–29	30	31
Antarctica: The Frozen Continent	32–33	34	35
Sarah's Choice	36–37	38	39
Metal Detector Detective	40–41	42	43
Growing Vegetables	44–45	46	47
Colonial New England	48–49	50	51
Gardening with Grandpa	52–53	54	55
The Elk Hunters	56–57	58	59
Paws and Claws: Learn About Animal Tracks	60–61	62	63
Rescuing Stranded Whales	64–65	66	67
Do Animals Have a Sixth Sense?	68–69	70	71
The Lesson of Icarus	72–73	74	75
Measuring the Weather	76–77	78	79
The Rock Kit	80–81	82	83

© Pearson Education

Graphic Organizers

Introduction

Scott Foresman *Reading Street* provides over 600 leveled readers that help children become better readers and build a lifelong love of reading. The *Reading Street* leveled readers are engaging texts that help children practice critical reading skills and strategies. They also provide opportunities to build vocabulary, understand concepts, and develop reading fluency.

The leveled readers were developed to be age-appropriate and appealing to children at each grade level. The leveled readers consist of engaging texts in a variety of genres, including fantasy, folk tales, realistic fiction, historical fiction, and narrative and expository nonfiction. To better address real-life reading skills that children will encounter in testing situations and beyond, a higher percentage of nonfiction texts is provided at each grade.

USING THE LEVELED READERS

You can use the leveled readers to meet the diverse needs of your children. Consider using the readers to

- practice critical skills and strategies
- build fluency
- build vocabulary and concepts
- build background for the main selections in the student book
- provide a variety of reading experiences, e.g., shared, group, individual, take-home, readers' theater

GUIDED READING APPROACH

The *Reading Street* leveled readers are leveled according to Guided Reading criteria by experts trained in Guided Reading. The Guided Reading levels increase in difficulty within a grade level and across grade levels. In addition to leveling according to Guided Reading criteria, the instruction provided in the *Leveled Reader Teaching Guide* is compatible with Guided Reading instruction. An instructional routine is provided for each leveled reader. This routine is most effective when working with individual children or small groups.

MANAGING THE CLASSROOM

When using the leveled readers with individuals or small groups, you'll want to keep the other children engaged in meaningful, independent learning tasks. Establishing independent work stations throughout the classroom and child routines for these work stations can help you manage the rest of the class while you work with individuals or small groups. Possible work stations include Listening, Phonics, Vocabulary, Independent Reading, and Cross-Curricular. For classroom management, create a work board that lists the work stations and which children should be at each station. Provide instructions at each station that detail the tasks to be accomplished. Update the board and alert children when they should rotate to a new station. For additional support for managing your classroom, see the *Reading Street Centers Survival Kit*.

USING THE LEVELED READER TEACHING GUIDE

The *Leveled Reader Teaching Guide* provides an instruction plan for each leveled reader based on the same instructional routine.

INTRODUCE THE BOOK The Introduction includes suggestions for creating interest in the text by discussing the title and author, building background, and previewing the book and its features.

READ THE BOOK Before students begin reading the book, have them set purposes for reading and discuss how they can use the reading strategy as they read. Determine how you want students in a particular group to read the text, softly or silently, to a specific point or the entire text. Then use the Comprehension Questions to provide support as needed and to assess comprehension.

REVISIT THE BOOK The Reader Response questions provide opportunities for students to demonstrate their understanding of the text, the target comprehension skill, and vocabulary. The Response Options require students to revisit the text to respond to what they've read and to move beyond the text to explore related content.

SKILL WORK The Skill Work box provides instruction and practice for the target skill and strategy and selection vocabulary. Instruction for an alternate comprehension skill allows teachers to provide additional skill instruction and practice for students.

USING THE GRAPHIC ORGANIZERS

Graphic organizers in blackline-master format can be found on pages 132–152. These can be used as overhead transparencies or as student worksheets.

ASSESSING PERFORMANCE

Use the assessment forms that begin on page 6 to make notes about your students' reading skills, use of reading strategies, and general reading behaviors.

MEASURE FLUENT READING (pp. 6–7) Provides directions for measuring a student's fluency, based on words correct per minute (wcpm), and reading accuracy using a running record.

OBSERVATION CHECKLIST (p. 8) Allows you to note the regularity with which students demonstrate their understanding and use of reading skills and strategies.

STUDENT SELF-ASSESSMENT (p. 9) Helps students identify their own areas of strength and areas where they need further work. This form (About My Reading) encourages them to list steps they can take to become better readers and to set goals as readers. Suggest that students share their self-assessment notes with their families so that family members can work with them more effectively to practice their reading skills and strategies at home.

READING STRATEGY ASSESSMENT (p. 10) Provides criteria for evaluating each student's proficiency as a strategic reader.

PROGRESS REPORT (p. 11) Provides a means to track a student's book-reading progress over a period of time by noting the level at which a student reads and his or her accuracy at that level. Reading the chart from left to right gives you a visual model of how quickly a student is making the transition from one level to the next. Share these reports with parents or guardians to help them see how their child's reading is progressing.

Measure Fluent Reading

Taking a Running Record

A running record is an assessment of a student's oral reading accuracy and oral reading fluency. Reading accuracy is based on the number of words read correctly. Reading fluency is based on the reading rate (the number of words correct per minute) and the degree to which a student reads with a "natural flow."

How to Measure Reading Accuracy

1. Choose a grade-level text of about 80 to 120 words that is unfamiliar to the student.
2. Make a copy of the text for yourself. Make a copy for the student or have the student read aloud from a book.
3. Give the student the text and have the student read aloud. (You may wish to record the student's reading for later evaluation.)
4. On your copy of the text, mark any miscues or errors the student makes while reading. See the running record sample on page 7, which shows how to identify and mark miscues.
5. Count the total number of words in the text and the total number of errors made by the student. Note: If a student makes the same error more than once, such as mispronouncing the same word multiple times, count it as one error. Self-corrections do not count as actual errors. Use the following formula to calculate the percentage score, or accuracy rate:

$$\frac{\text{Total Number of Words} - \text{Total Number of Errors}}{\text{Total Number of Words}} \times 100 = \text{percentage score}$$

Interpreting the Results

- A student who reads **95–100%** of the words correctly is reading at an **independent level** and may need more challenging text.
- A student who reads **90–94%** of the words correctly is reading at an **instructional level** and will likely benefit from guided instruction.
- A student who reads **89%** or fewer of the words correctly is reading at a **frustrational level** and may benefit most from targeted instruction with lower-level texts and intervention.

How to Measure Reading Rate (WCPM)

1. Follow Steps 1–3 above.
2. Note the exact times when the student begins and finishes reading.
3. Use the following formula to calculate the number of words correct per minute (WCPM):

$$\frac{\text{Total Number of Words Read Correctly}}{\text{Total Number of Seconds}} \times 60 = \text{words correct per minute}$$

Interpreting the Results

By the end of the year, a third-grader should be reading approximately 110–120 WCPM.

Running Record Sample

Running Record Sample

> Dana had recently begun volunteering at the animal rescue shelter where her mom worked as a veterinarian. The shelter was (just) across the bay from their house.
>
> Dana was learning many different [H] jobs at the shelter. She fed the dogs and cleaned their cages. She played catch with the dogs in the shelter's backyard. Dana's favorite job /jōb/, however, was introducing people to the dogs waiting for adoption. Whenever a dog found a new home, Dana was especially (SC) pleased!
>
> The road to the shelter crossed over the bay. Dana looked for ^the boats in the channel, but there were none. Dana's mom turned on the radio to ~~listen~~ hear to the news as they drove. The weather reporter announced that a blizzard might hit some parts of the state.
>
> —From *A Day with the Dogs*
> On-Level Reader 3.3.4

Notations

Accurate Reading
The student reads a word correctly.

Omission
The student omits words or word parts.

Hesitation
The student hesitates over a word, and the teacher provides the word. Wait several seconds before telling the student what the word is.

Mispronunciation/Misreading
The student pronounces or reads a word incorrectly.

Self-correction
The student reads a word incorrectly but then corrects the error. Do not count self-corrections as actual errors. However, noting self-corrections will help you identify words the student finds difficult.

Insertion
The student inserts words or parts of words that are not in the text.

Substitution
The student substitutes words or parts of words for the words in the text.

Running Record Results
Total Number of Words: **126**
Number of Errors: **5**

Reading Time: **64 seconds**

▶ **Reading Accuracy**
$$\frac{126 - 5}{126} \times 100 = 96.032 = 96\%$$

Accuracy Percentage Score: **96%**

▶ **Reading Rate—WCPM**
$$\frac{121}{64} \times 60 = 113.44 = 113 \text{ words correct per minute}$$

Reading Rate: **113 WCPM**

Observation Checklist

Student's Name _____ Date _____

Behaviors Observed	Always (Proficient)	Usually (Fluent)	Sometimes (Developing)	Rarely (Novice)
Reading Strategies and Skills				
Uses prior knowledge and preview to understand what book is about				
Makes predictions and checks them while reading				
Uses context clues to figure out meanings of new words				
Uses phonics and syllabication to decode words				
Self-corrects while reading				
Reads at an appropriate reading rate				
Reads with appropriate intonation and stress				
Uses fix-up strategies				
Identifies story elements: character, setting, plot, theme				
Summarizes plot or main ideas accurately				
Uses target comprehension skill to understand the text better				
Responds thoughtfully about the text				
Reading Behaviors and Attitudes				
Enjoys listening to stories				
Chooses reading as a free-time activity				
Reads with sustained interest and attention				
Participates in discussion about books				

General Comments

About My Reading

Name _____ Date _____

1. **Compared with earlier in the year, I am enjoying reading**

   ☐ more   ☐ less   ☐ about the same

2. **When I read now, I understand**

   ☐ more than I used to   ☐ about the same as I used to

3. **One thing that has helped me with my reading is**

   _____

   _____

   _____

4. **One thing that could make me a better reader is**

   _____

   _____

   _____

5. **Here is one selection or book that I really enjoyed reading:**

   _____

   _____

6. **Here are some reasons why I liked it:**

   _____

   _____

   _____

   _____

   _____

   _____

Reading Strategy Assessment

Student _____ Date _____

Teacher _____

		Proficient	Developing	Emerging	Not showing trait
Building Background Comments:	Previews	☐	☐	☐	☐
	Asks questions	☐	☐	☐	☐
	Predicts	☐	☐	☐	☐
	Activates prior knowledge	☐	☐	☐	☐
	Sets own purposes for reading	☐	☐	☐	☐
	Other:	☐	☐	☐	☐
Comprehension Comments:	Retells/summarizes	☐	☐	☐	☐
	Questions, evaluates ideas	☐	☐	☐	☐
	Relates to self/other texts	☐	☐	☐	☐
	Paraphrases	☐	☐	☐	☐
	Rereads/reads ahead for meaning	☐	☐	☐	☐
	Visualizes	☐	☐	☐	☐
	Uses decoding strategies	☐	☐	☐	☐
	Uses vocabulary strategies	☐	☐	☐	☐
	Understands key ideas of a text	☐	☐	☐	☐
	Other:	☐	☐	☐	☐
Fluency Comments:	Adjusts reading rate	☐	☐	☐	☐
	Reads for accuracy	☐	☐	☐	☐
	Uses expression	☐	☐	☐	☐
	Other:	☐	☐	☐	☐
Connections Comments:	Relates text to self	☐	☐	☐	☐
	Relates text to text	☐	☐	☐	☐
	Relates text to world	☐	☐	☐	☐
	Other:	☐	☐	☐	☐
Self-Assessment Comments:	Is aware of: Strengths	☐	☐	☐	☐
	Needs	☐	☐	☐	☐
	Improvement/achievement	☐	☐	☐	☐
	Sets and implements learning goals	☐	☐	☐	☐
	Maintains logs, records, portfolio	☐	☐	☐	☐
	Works with others	☐	☐	☐	☐
	Shares ideas and materials	☐	☐	☐	☐
	Other:	☐	☐	☐	☐

Progress Report

Student's Name _____

At the top of the chart, record the book title, its grade/unit/week (for example, 1.2.3), and the student's accuracy percentage. See page 6 for measuring fluency, calculating accuracy and reading rates. At the bottom of the chart, record the date you took the running record. In the middle of the chart, make an X in the box across from the level of the student's reading—frustrational level (below 89% accuracy), instructional level (90–94% accuracy), or independent level (95–100% accuracy). Record the reading rate (WCPM) in the next row.

Book Title					
Grade/Unit/Week					
Reading Accuracy Percentage					
LEVEL — Frustrational (89% or below)					
LEVEL — Instructional (90–94%)					
LEVEL — Independent (95% or above)					
Reading Rate (WCPM)					
Date					

The California Gold Rush: A Letter Home

SUMMARY A boy named Josh is thrilled when he receives a letter from his Uncle Zach, who has moved to California with dreams of finding gold and making a fortune. However, the letter reveals that the Gold Rush is not what Zach and other miners from around the world had hoped it would be.

LESSON VOCABULARY

boom	coins
fetched	laundry
mending	pick
skillet	spell

INTRODUCE THE BOOK

INTRODUCE THE TITLE AND AUTHOR Discuss with students the title and the author of *The California Gold Rush: A Letter Home*. Ask them to look at the cover photo and talk about how it might relate to the title. Ask: Who are the men pictured in the photo? What are they looking at? Why are they looking?

BUILD BACKGROUND Discuss reasons why people might decide to move from one part of the country to another. Ask students if they have ever moved from one area to another or if they know of people who have. Did they ever get messages from them? If so, what did the messages reveal?

ELL Tell students that this story focuses on a letter written from California. Point out California on a map, and use pictures from books or artifacts such as postcards to tell more about it.

PREVIEW/USE TEXT FEATURES Have students preview the book by looking at the illustrations and photos. Point out the unique way in which italicized text is presented on certain pages along with photos. Why might the author have chosen this arrangement? How might it relate to the book's title?

READ THE BOOK

SET PURPOSE Have students set a purpose for reading *The California Gold Rush: A Letter Home*. Invite them to ask questions about the title, such as, "What was the California Gold Rush?" They may also think about circumstances under which people write letters to families back home. Students' curiosity about these matters should guide their purpose.

STRATEGY SUPPORT: PRIOR KNOWLEDGE Remind students that prior knowledge is what they know about a given topic. Prior knowledge includes other readings and other experiences one might have had outside the classroom. Survey readers' prior knowledge of the topic by asking questions to identify areas of weakness. These areas may indicate a lack of familiarity with important concepts that might jeopardize a thorough understanding of the book. Help struggling students develop more prior knowledge before reading by providing additional information about the California Gold Rush.

COMPREHENSION QUESTIONS

PAGES 4–5 What parts of Zach's letter tell you this a realistic story? *(It was written in California in 1850, a real time and place in history.)*

PAGE 7 At first, how do Zach and other miners search for gold? *(They use picks to loosen rocks and dirt from the bottom of a river and then put the dirt into pans for careful sorting.)*

PAGE 11 How do you think Josh's family will feel after Pa reads the letter? *(Possible response: They may be disappointed that Zach's dreams of gold did not come true but happy that he will be returning home.)*

REVISIT THE BOOK

READER RESPONSE

1. It is a realistic story.
2. Answers will vary based on what students have read and experienced.
3. Possible response: The fireworks make a loud boom.
4. Possible response: No, because he is disappointed that they had not found much gold.

EXTEND UNDERSTANDING Invite students to examine closely the use of photographs and illustrations in the book. Ask: How does their usage differ, and why might the author have chosen to use them in different ways? If illustrations of gold rush miners were used instead of photos, how might your thoughts about the book change?

RESPONSE OPTIONS

WRITING Ask students to pretend they are members of Zach's family and are writing letters in response to the one he sent. They should write about their feelings and describe their own lives at home during the 1850s.

WORD WORK Help students sort vocabulary words related to different aspects of life during the California Gold Rush by creating categories such as *location, jobs, equipment,* and so on.

SOCIAL STUDIES CONNECTION

Time For **SOCIAL STUDIES**

Have students use reference materials to learn more about modern-day California. Then ask them to use their information to pick a location in California and pretend they are there writing a letter to a friend.

Skill Work

TEACH/REVIEW VOCABULARY

Read the vocabulary words. Ask students about words they may already know. Discuss how they first heard of the words and what they think the words mean. Tell them that they will become more familiar with these words as they read.

TARGET SKILL AND STRATEGY

REALISM AND FANTASY Tell students that a *realistic story* tells about something that could happen while a *fantasy* is a story about something that could not happen. Ask students to point out specific elements of *The California Gold Rush* that indicate what type of story it is.

PRIOR KNOWLEDGE Tell students that *prior knowledge* is what they know about a given topic. Prior knowledge might be gathered from their reading and personal experiences. Explain that connecting prior knowledge to text can help students understand what they read. Read aloud sections of the book and pause to ask students what it reminds them of. Tell them to think of their own lives; previously read books; and people, places, and things in the world. Remind students that readers can use their prior knowledge to determine whether a story is a realistic story or a fantasy. Invite them to point out how previously read books and their own life experiences suggest what type of story is told in *The California Gold Rush*.

ADDITIONAL SKILL INSTRUCTION

DRAW CONCLUSIONS When students *draw conclusions,* they should use what they read and what they already know to figure out more than what is presented in the book. Use graphic organizers to model how to draw conclusions, such as a chart with columns for facts from the book, what one already knows, and the conclusions that result. Have students share facts and prior knowledge while drawing conclusions about what they read in the book.

Realism and Fantasy

- A **realistic story** tells about something that could happen.
- A **fantasy** is a story about something that could not happen.

Directions Read each sentence below. Write *R* on the line if it comes from a realistic story or *F* if it comes from a fantasy.

1. _____ People used picks, shovels, and pans in their search for gold in California.

2. _____ Workers from across America flew to California on golden geese when the Gold Rush began in 1849.

3. _____ People from all over the world traveled to San Francisco with hopes of striking it rich.

4. _____ Nuggets of gold were found buried in dirt and growing on trees during the California Gold Rush.

5. _____ Miners took baths in rivers when they were not busy searching for gold.

6. _____ At the very beginning of the Gold Rush, people could find gold simply by looking down into rivers.

7. _____ Parts of the sun sometimes break off and fall to Earth as nuggets of gold.

8. _____ News of the California Gold Rush spread quickly through newspapers and television.

Vocabulary

Directions Choose the word from the box that best matches each definition.
Write the word on the line.

Check the Words You Know

___ boom	___ coins
___ fetched	___ laundry
___ mending	___ pick
___ skillet	___ spell

1. _____ a heavy tool used to break up soil or rocks

2. _____ fixing or repairing

3. _____ a big increase in size or number

4. _____ a period of time

5. _____ a frying pan

6. _____ pieces of metal used as money

7. _____ clothing set aside for washing

8. _____ brought back

Directions Select three vocabulary words and write a sentence using each one.

9. _____

_____

10. _____

_____

11. _____

_____

It's A Fair Swap!

SUMMARY This nonfiction book describes bartering in early America and how, as the country grew, bartering gave way to the use of paper money.

LESSON VOCABULARY

carpenter	carpetmaker
knowledge	marketplace
merchant	plenty
straying	thread

INTRODUCE THE BOOK

INTRODUCE THE TITLE AND AUTHOR Introduce students to the title and the author of the book *It's A Fair Swap!* Based on the title, ask students what kind of information they think this book will provide. Ask students what they think the people in the cover illustration are doing and why they are doing it.

BUILD BACKGROUND Invite students to consider how they would get the things they wanted or needed if there was no money in the world. Ask students if they have ever traded or swapped something for something else. Tell students that this is called *bartering,* an act they will read and learn about in the book.

PREVIEW/USE TEXT FEATURES Invite students to take a picture walk through the illustrations. Ask students how the illustrations give clues to what the book might be about. Direct students' attention to page 12 and the thought balloon drawn over the girl's head. Ask: What do you think is happening in this particular photograph? How might it relate to the topic of the book?

READ THE BOOK

SET PURPOSE Have students set a purpose for reading *It's A Fair Swap!* Students' curiosity about swapping and bartering should guide this purpose. Suggest that students think about the necessity for bartering as they read the book.

STRATEGY SUPPORT: SUMMARIZE As students read the book, suggest that they write down and number the major ideas and milestones. After reading, have students write summary paragraphs using their notes as guides.

COMPREHENSION QUESTIONS

PAGE 4 What is the sequence of events in a barter? *(People decide what they want to trade, approach another person and determine if the goods have equal value, and either make the trade or not.)*

PAGE 4 In bartering, what must both people agree on? *(People must agree that their goods have equal value.)*

PAGE 5 Why didn't the colonists use European money in America? *(There were no stores or banks.)*

PAGE 9 Why did the farmers need to grow extra crops? *(Farmers used these extra crops to barter for things they couldn't make or grow.)*

PAGE 10 Why did the colonists start using paper money? *(It was easier to carry than crops or livestock.)*

PAGE 12 Why do you think bartering still goes on today? *(Possible responses: people do not always have money; bartering is fun.)*

REVISIT THE BOOK

READER RESPONSE

1. Correct sequence: Colonists plant or hunt their own food; the barter system is used at the general store; people begin using money to buy things from their local merchants; shopping malls replace the general stores.
2. The general store was important because it sold or bartered everything that couldn't be grown or made on a farm.
3. *know*; possible response: I know that Boston is the capital of Massachusetts.
4. Possible responses: candles, paper, books

EXTEND UNDERSTANDING Remind students that the *setting* is where and when a story takes place. Discuss with students the settings covered in pages 4–19 of *It's A Fair Swap!* Ask: Why were these particular settings conducive to bartering? Is bartering as necessary in a modern city as it was in the colonial period? Why or why not?

RESPONSE OPTIONS

WRITING Remind students that in bartering, the more valuable an item you have to trade, the more valuable an item you are likely to get in return. With this in mind, ask students to write a script for a commercial for an item they want to barter. Suggest that they use persuasive language. Ask volunteers to present their commercials to the class.

SOCIAL STUDIES CONNECTION

Time For **SOCIAL STUDIES**

Hand out large sheets of paper and have students divide them in half. On the left side of their papers, students should draw or paste pictures of something they want to barter. On the right side, have students draw or paste pictures of items they think might be of equal value.

Skill Work

TEACH/REVIEW VOCABULARY

After reviewing the vocabulary words with students, play Vocabulary Master. Give students a list of definitions and have them match each definition to the appropriate vocabulary word. Then have students use each word in a sentence.

ELL Write *marketplace* on the board and have students identify the two words that form this compound. Discuss how you can arrive at a definition for *marketplace* by combining the meanings of *market* and *place*. Finally have students contribute other words they know that are formed with *place* (*someplace, misplace, birthplace,* etc.).

TARGET SKILL AND STRATEGY

SEQUENCE Remind students that the *sequence* is the order in which events happen. Ask students to tell the sequence of events of getting to school each morning or of doing their homework. To further illustrate the concept, have students number each event so they can see the sequence of events more easily.

SUMMARIZE Remind students that *summarizing* is reducing what you have read into the most important ideas. It can help you understand the main points of a story. Ask students to summarize a familiar story like *The Three Bears*.

ADDITIONAL SKILL INSTRUCTION

FACT AND OPINION Remind students that a *statement of fact* is a statement which can be proved true or false and a *statement of opinion* is a belief that cannot be proved true or false. Invite students to tell you a few facts about school. Then ask for a few opinions. Discuss the difference.

Sequence

Sequence of events in a story is the order in which the events occur.

Directions To help you understand the sequence of events in *It's A Fair Swap!* use this flow chart. It is called a flow chart because one event "flows" into another, from first to last. Reread the story. As you read, answer the questions.

1. What happened **first?**
   _____
   _____
   _____

2. What happened **next?**
   _____
   _____
   _____

3. What happened **after that?**
   _____
   _____
   _____

4. What was the **last** thing that happened?
   _____
   _____
   _____

Vocabulary

Directions Unscramble each vocabulary word and write the word on the line.
Then fit each vocabulary word into the right sentence.

Check the Words You Know

___carpenter   ___carpetmaker   ___knowledge   ___marketplace
___merchant   ___plenty   ___straying   ___thread

1. racpeetnr   _____

2. gdnwoklee   _____

3. ketplmarace   _____

4. tylpen   _____

5. ingtsray   _____

6. raedth   _____

7. erpetcarkam   _____

8. chentmar   _____

9. The _____ built us a wonderful table.

10. I need to sew this button on my shirt, so please bring me a needle and
_____ .

11. That dog is not staying close to home but is _____ .

12. There is lots of food, so there will be _____ to eat.

13. The _____ sells apples, oranges, and pears.

14. An encyclopedia contains lots of _____ .

15. This rug needs repair, so we must call the _____ .

16. The _____ sells many delicious fruits and vegetables.

Directions Write two sentences, using a vocabulary word in each.

17. _____

_____

18. _____

_____

Making Sense of Dollars and Cents

SUMMARY In this nonfiction book, students are introduced to budget basics, including the steps in making a budget, how to determine income and expenses, and how to calculate a deficit or surplus.

LESSON VOCABULARY

college	dimes
downtown	fined
nickels	quarters
rich	

INTRODUCE THE BOOK

INTRODUCE THE TITLE AND AUTHOR Discuss with students the title and the author of *Making Sense of Dollars and Cents*. Make sure students understand the difference between *sense* and *cents*. Point out that the words are *homonyms*, words that sound the same but have different spellings and meanings.

ELL Have students distinguish between *sense* and *cents* by drawing pictures that illustrate the meanings of the words.

BUILD BACKGROUND Point out to students that *dollars* and *cents* are types of money. Without using the terms *income* or *expenses*, ask students if they ever have their own money to spend. Discuss where they get their money and what they spend it on.

PREVIEW/USE TEXT FEATURES Have students look at the illustrations on the cover and inside the book. Discuss with students what the children in the pictures appear to be doing. Talk about the familiar objects in the pictures, such as a pencil, pad of paper, calculator, toys, a piggy bank. Invite students to tell what these pictures have in common with the words *dollars* and *cents*.

READ THE BOOK

SET PURPOSE Help students set their own purposes for reading the book. Ask: What would you like to learn about money? *(For example: how to make money, how to save money, how to open a bank account)* Suggest that students look for information about these topics as they read.

STRATEGY SUPPORT: VISUALIZE To support students' visualizations at the end of each page, have them write words from the text that create mental pictures of what is happening.

COMPREHENSION QUESTIONS

PAGE 3 Visualize the different ways you spend money. What do you spend your money on? *(Possible response: candy bars, comic books, school supplies)*

PAGES 5–6 What is income? What are expenses? *(Income is money you receive. Expenses are things you spend money on.)*

PAGES 8–9 Make a generalization about deficits. *(All deficits are bad.)*

PAGES 11–12 List the sequence for budgeting your money. *(First, separate income into three envelopes marked* expenses, spending, *and* saving. *Then find ways to earn money. Last, start saving.)*

REVISIT THE BOOK

READER RESPONSE

1. Possible responses: total income, total expenses, total surplus or deficit

2. Possible responses: I saw myself raking leaves for a neighbor. It made what I was reading seem real.

3. Possible response: I ate a very *rich* dessert last night.

4. Possible response: to add, subtract, multiply, and divide numbers

EXTEND UNDERSTANDING Once students have read the book, discuss how the illustrations in the book helped them understand the text. Discuss whether the illustrations helped students visualize what was being discussed, even when there were no actions or descriptions.

RESPONSE OPTIONS

WRITING Ask students to think of a time when their expenses were greater than their incomes, such as when they wanted to buy something special but didn't have enough money. Have students write a sequence of events describing the situation. What did they do about it?

MATHEMATICS CONNECTION

Using real or imaginary income and expenses, have students create their own budgets that show a total surplus or deficit. Students can exchange their budgets with partners, who will look for ways to cut deficits or reduce spending.

Skill Work

TEACH/REVIEW VOCABULARY

Have groups use dictionaries to define the vocabulary words and identify their parts of speech. Then have groups create as many categories as possible into which they can sort the words (for example, *Nouns*, *Plural Words*, *Types of Money*, *Places You Can Go*). Ask groups to share the definitions and categories with the class.

ELL Have pairs of students write the vocabulary words on index cards, and place the cards facedown in a pile. One person picks a card and acts out the word until his or her partner guesses it. The partner has as many guesses as necessary. Pairs try to see who can guess the most words correctly.

TARGET SKILL AND STRATEGY

SEQUENCE Review with students that a *sequence* is the order in which events happen. Remind students that sometimes an author uses clue words such as *first*, *next*, *then*, and *last* to show sequence. Have students look for sequence clue words as they read.

VISUALIZE Review with students that when they *visualize,* they make a mental picture of what is happening in a selection. Tell students that visualizing information can help them better understand the sequence of events in a selection. Suggest that at the end of every page, students visualize what they have just read.

ADDITIONAL SKILL INSTRUCTION

GENERALIZE Explain to students that when they read, they sometimes can make a *generalization* about several things or people as a group. This statement may be about how the ideas are mostly alike or all alike. As an example, tell students that you can make a statement about how all birds are alike by saying, "All birds have feathers." As they read, have students think of a statement that shows how some ideas in the book are alike.

Sequence

- **Sequence** is the order in which things happen in a story or selection—
  what happens first, next, and last.

Directions Read the following passage. Then complete the story sequence chart below.

John was excited because he was going to the mall with his friends after school. He had saved $10 of his allowance money.

At 2:30 P.M., John met his friends outside. First, they walked five blocks to the shopping mall. Then they all went straight to the bookstore. John and his friends grabbed the last copies of their favorite comic books.

John and his friends went to the cash register. John felt in his pocket for his ten dollars. The book cost $9.58 with tax. But two dollars were missing from his money! What would he do? Luckily his friends put their money together and gave him the extra he needed.

1–3. What happened at the end of the school day?

First, _____

_____

Next, _____

_____

Then, _____

_____

4–6. What happened at the bookstore?

First, _____

_____

Next, _____

_____

Last, _____

_____

REVISIT THE BOOK

READER RESPONSE

1. Possible response: It is realistic for a boy to want a dog, get a job delivering newspapers, and earn enough money to buy the dog.
2. Step 1: ten quarters = $2.50
   Step 2: seven dimes = 70¢
   Step 3: eleven nickels = 55¢
   Step 4: thirty-seven pennies = 37¢
   Step 5 = $2.50 + $0.70 + $0.55 + $0.37 = $4.12
3. Possible response: the money paid for the use of someone else's money
4. Possible response: I would do chores for my family and neighbors.

EXTEND UNDERSTANDING

Ask students to look at the illustrations where Davis is looking up on page 3. Explain that the drawings show that Davis is thinking and dreaming about dogs. Ask: Could this really happen?

RESPONSE OPTIONS

WORD WORK On page 10 Davis wishes he had a million dollars to buy dog toys. Ask: Do you think Davis would need that much money? Have students complete the following sentences with words that make each statement an exaggeration: *I'm so hungry, I could eat _____! This meat is as tough as _____. I could watch that movie _____ times!*

SOCIAL STUDIES CONNECTION

Time For **SOCIAL STUDIES**

Explain to students that something you *need* is something that is necessary to live, such as food, clothing, and shelter. Something you *want* is a desire. Ask: For Davis, was the dog a need or a want? Have students make lists of things they would like to have. Have them sort them into needs and wants.

Skill Work

TEACH/REVIEW VOCABULARY

Have students work in pairs with a set of vocabulary word cards. One student picks a card and defines the word while the partner uses it in a sentence. Then have partners switch roles as they draw another card.

TARGET SKILL AND STRATEGY

REALISM AND FANTASY Remind students that *realistic stories* and *fantasies* are both "made up." However, a realistic story tells about something that could happen, while a fantasy is a story about something that could not happen. On the board, write: *The dog read the paper. The boy sold lemonade.* Ask: Which one of these sentences is realistic? Which one is a fantasy?

MONITOR AND FIX UP Remind students that they should *monitor* their understanding of a story as they read. Tell them that when a story stops making sense, there are things they can do to *fix up* any problems they have with understanding it. For example, they can take notes to keep track of what happens in the story, or they can read on to find out if something that is confusing is cleared up later. Remind students that if they fix up any comprehension problem they have, it will be easier to determine if the story is a realistic story or a fantasy.

ADDITIONAL SKILL INSTRUCTION

MAIN IDEA As they read the story, ask students to question what it is about—its *main idea.* Tell students to look for details in the text that support their answers. Model: "What is page 9 about? I think it is about Davis saving more and more money. The details that support my answer are that Davis gets checks for delivering newspapers, he puts his money in the bank, and every month the interest grows."

Name _____

Realism and Fantasy

- A **realistic story** tells about something that could happen.
- A **fantasy** is a story about something that could not happen.

Directions Read the selection from *Davis Buys a Dog*. Then answer the questions that follow.

> Davis saw a sign on his way home from school. The corner store needed someone to deliver newspapers on Saturdays. *I can do that!* Davis thought. "Mom! I can deliver newspapers to earn money!" Davis shouted. "Now I can get a dog of my own!"
>
> So Davis delivered newspapers on Saturdays. Mom followed on her bicycle.

1. Could things in this story really happen?

   Write *Yes* or *No*. _____

   Write a detail from the selection that supports your answer. _____

   _____

2. Do the people in the selection do things like people you know?

   Write *Yes* or *No*. _____

   Write a detail from the selection that supports your answer. _____

   _____

3. Do the people in the selection say or think things like people you know?

   Write *Yes* or *No*. _____

   Write a detail from the selection that supports your answer. _____

   _____

4. Is this selection a realistic story or a fantasy? Write an *X* next to the correct answer.

   realistic story _____   fantasy _____

Vocabulary

Directions Unscramble each word from the box. Then write its definition.

Check the Words You Know

___amount   ___check   ___earn
___expensive   ___interest   ___million
___thousand   ___value   ___worth

1. ountam _____

   _____

2. nrea _____

   _____

3. kcehc _____

   _____

4. nimilol _____

   _____

5. dsathuon _____

   _____

Directions Complete each sentence. Fill in each blank with the best word from the box.

6. Davis thought that a dog was _____ all the hard work that he did.

7. Davis had to earn more money, because the dog was too _____ .

8. At first, the _____ of money Davis had was only $4.12.

9. Davis kept his money in the bank and earned one dollar in _____ .

10. After getting his dog, Davis knew the _____ of hard work.

E-Pals

SUMMARY This is a book about two friends from very different cultures and how they keep in touch via e-mail. Through the characters' messages, students can see the differences and similarities in these friends' values and in their cultures. Students can also experience storytelling in a new way—through e-mails.

LESSON VOCABULARY

arranged	bundles
dangerously	errands
excitedly	steady
unwrapped	wobbled

INTRODUCE THE BOOK

INTRODUCE THE TITLE AND AUTHOR Discuss with students the title and the author of *E-Pals*. Based on the title, ask students what kind of information they think this book will provide. Ask: Have you ever read a book in e-mail form?

BUILD BACKGROUND Discuss with students if they have ever written letters or sent e-mails to friends or pen pals. Ask: What sorts of things did you write about? Do students know people from different countries? Discuss how they think students from different countries might differ from and be similar to students in the classroom.

PREVIEW/USE ILLUSTRATIONS Have students preview the book by looking at the illustrations. Ask: Where do you think these two e-pals live? (*The girl probably lives in the United States, and the boy lives in Africa.*)

READ THE BOOK

SET PURPOSE Have students set a purpose for reading *E-Pals*. Students' curiosity about different countries and their interest in e-mail and computers should guide this purpose.

STRATEGY SUPPORT: STORY STRUCTURE As students read about the two friends getting to know each other, they should follow the story structure to help them keep track of its overall meaning. Following a story from beginning to end will help students distinguish between plot and detail. The story is easy to follow in this book because the actions and ideas are divided into e-mail messages. If you wish, explain to students that telling a story through letters is a very old form of story structure. Ask if students think e-mail is equally old. (*No, because computers, and therefore e-mail, have only been around for a comparatively few years.*)

COMPREHENSION QUESTIONS

PAGES 4–5 What are the two main settings in this book? (*Tanzania and Colorado*)

PAGE 6 What is similar about Tanzania and Colorado? (*Possible responses: Soccer is enjoyed in both places; both have wildlife.*)

PAGES 6–7 What does Molly put in her message that makes Juma answer? (*a question*)

PAGES 10–11 How is Molly going to try and make Juma's visit fun? (*Juma wants to see grizzlies, and Molly's father is going to take them to the mountains to look for wildlife.*)

REVISIT THE BOOK

READER RESPONSE

1. Possible responses: Juma is friendly and generous. He e-mails Molly and sends her a carved giraffe; he plays soccer and is athletic; he is responsible because he helps his father.
2. Molly writes to Juma about the giraffe. Juma writes about his father's tour and soccer. Molly writes about American sports and the Fourth of July. Juma writes about a baby zebra.
3. *Excitedly* means "with strong, lively feelings." *Dangerously* means "not safely."
4. Responses will vary.

EXTEND UNDERSTANDING Discuss with students how *plot* refers to the events of the story and always has a beginning, middle, and end. Suggest that students look at both the beginning and the ending of the story and then discuss with students whether Molly and Juma are better friends at the beginning of the story or at the end.

RESPONSE OPTIONS

WRITING Ask students what interests them about where Juma or Molly lives and what else they would like to know about the characters' lives. Then ask students to write e-mails to both Juma and Molly, asking them questions about their homes and their activities. Have volunteers read their e-mails aloud.

SOCIAL STUDIES CONNECTION

Time For SOCIAL STUDIES

Assign each student an imaginary pen pal from another country. Have students research what their e-pals' countries are like. Discuss the things students might like to ask their pen pals and the things they think their pen pals might like to know about life in the United States. Invite students to compose their letters in class. Create a bulletin board where students can post their letters.

Skill Work

TEACH/REVIEW VOCABULARY

Review the vocabulary words with students. Then play "right word, wrong sentence" with students. Take a word like *steady* and use it in two different sentences: *That strong table is steady. The tilted table with the broken leg is steady.* Then ask students to determine in which sentence the word is used correctly. *(the first)* Repeat with all vocabulary words.

TARGET SKILL AND STRATEGY

CHARACTER AND SETTING Remind students that *characters* are the people or animals that do the actions in a story. *Settings* are where the actions are done. Ask students to keep track of the characters and settings as they read. They may want to use a graphic organizer.

STORY STRUCTURE Remind students that the *story structure* is how a story is organized, and that a story has a beginning, a middle, and an end. Discuss with students how this story might look different from other stories they have read because it is written as a series of e-mails. Ask students to think about what the beginning, middle, and end might be as they read.

ELL Instruct students to write three different sentences. One sentence will describe the beginning of the story, one will describe the middle, and the last will describe the end.

ADDITIONAL SKILL INSTRUCTION

COMPARE AND CONTRAST Remind students that *comparing* means finding similarities between things and *contrasting* means finding differences. With students, make a chart that compares and contrasts the two characters from the book.

Name _____

Character and Setting

- **Characters** are the people or animals who do the action in a story.
- The **setting** is where the story takes place.

Directions Write the answers to the questions on the lines below.

1. Molly and Juma send a lot of e-mails to each other. What does this tell you about their characters?

_____

_____

_____

2. Why do you think Molly and Juma write each other about their countries?

_____

_____

_____

3. On pages 8 and 9 there is a mark of punctuation that shows Molly and Juma are excited. What is it?

_____

_____

4. What things in this story make you know that Molly and Juma are friends?

_____

_____

_____

5. The e-mails in this story do not have dates on them, but one of the e-mails gives clues to what time of year it is. What is the clue?

_____

_____

Vocabulary

Directions Fill in the letters to make each of the words from the box. Then write a definition on the line under the word.

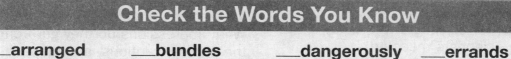

Check the Words You Know

___arranged	___bundles	___dangerously	___errands
___excitedly	___steady	___unwrapped	___wobbled

1. ___ R R ___ N ___ ___ D

_____

2. W ___ B B ___ ___ ___

_____

3. E ___ ___ A ___ D S

_____

4. E ___ C ___ ___ E ___ ___ Y

_____

5. ___ T ___ A D ___

_____

6. D ___ ___ G E ___ ___ ___ S ___ Y

_____

7. ___ U ___ D ___ E S

_____

8. ___ N ___ R ___ P P ___ ___

_____

Directions Write a sentence that includes one of the vocabulary words.

9. _____

_____

Antarctica: The Frozen Continent

SUMMARY Though Antarctica is the coldest place on Earth, it is home to penguins, seals, and other animals. Antarctica is also a fascinating place for scientists who study weather. These scientists measure temperature changes there to understand the effects of air pollution on global climates.

LESSON VOCABULARY

cuddles	flippers
frozen	hatch
pecks	preen
snuggles	

INTRODUCE THE BOOK

INTRODUCE THE TITLE AND AUTHOR Discuss with students the title and the author of *Antarctica: The Frozen Continent.* Ask: What does the cover photo tell you about Antarctica's climate, land, and animals? Discuss what information students think the author will provide based on the title and cover.

BUILD BACKGROUND Invite students to discuss what they know about Antarctica from movies, TV, books, or magazines. Ask: What might you see if you traveled to Antarctica? Does it seem like a place you would want to visit? Why or why not?

PREVIEW/USE TEXT FEATURES Have students look at the pictures, captions, and diagrams to find clues about what aspects of Antarctica will be covered in the book. Point out that certain images, such as snow and penguins, appear often in the pictures.

READ THE BOOK

SET PURPOSE Have students set a purpose for reading *Antarctica: The Frozen Continent.* What impressions do they get from skimming the photos, captions, and maps in the book? What makes Antarctica so different from most other continents? Students' curiosity should guide their purpose for reading.

STRATEGY SUPPORT: GRAPHIC ORGANIZERS Invite readers to keep track of their thinking by using *KWL* (*K*now, *W*ant to know, *L*earned) charts. Before reading, create a KWL chart on the board about Antarctica. Ask students to share what they already know about Antarctica and come up with questions about what they would like to know. During their reading, have students look for answers to their questions and tell what they have learned about Antarctica. Record all responses in the appropriate columns.

COMPREHENSION QUESTIONS

PAGE 5 What types of animals live in Antarctica? *(penguins, fish, seals, and whales)*

PAGES 6–8 What is the main idea of this section? *(Possible response: Scientists who study the weather in Antarctica use very specialized tools.)*

PAGE 9 How is Antarctica helping scientists learn about climate change? *(Possible response: Its changes in temperature tell about the effects of global warming.)*

REVISIT THE BOOK

READER RESPONSE

1. Possible response: Scientists study the climate in Antarctica as a way to protect the animals that live there.
2. Possible response: *Acoustic sounders*—send out beeping sounds whose echoes tell scientists about wind speed and direction; *Satellites*—send weather information to stations in Antarctica; *Weather balloons*—record information about air and send it back to weather stations in Antarctica through attached radios.
3. The words that follow—"or clean and smooth their feathers"—show what *preen* means.
4. Responses will vary.

EXTEND UNDERSTANDING Point out how images in the book are paired together for certain reasons. Ask students what they can learn from such combinations, such as the satellite image paired with the photo of an actual satellite on page 7 and the global warming diagram paired with the photo of a traffic jam on page 9.

RESPONSE OPTIONS

WRITING Ask students to pretend they are visiting Antarctica and writing letters to friends at home. Have them write one or two paragraphs describing their experiences.

WORD WORK On the board, write groups of four words, three of which have similar meanings and one of which is completely opposite or unrelated. Include story vocabulary words in some groups. Have students point out which word in each group does not belong. For example, in the group *frozen, icy, freezing,* and *melted*, the word *melted* does not belong.

SCIENCE CONNECTION

Scientists in Antarctica use special equipment to gather information. Invite students to learn how scientists in other environments use special tools and technology to gather information.

TIME FOR
Science

Skill Work

TEACH/REVIEW VOCABULARY

Discuss the vocabulary words and reinforce word meaning by asking questions such as, "What are some animals that have *flippers?*"

ELL Distribute index cards, each with a vocabulary word written on it. Challenge students to go on a scavenger hunt to find books, magazines, or other print sources containing the same word.

TARGET SKILL AND STRATEGY

MAIN IDEA Remind students that the *main idea* is the most important idea about a topic. *Supporting details* are pieces of information that tell more about the main idea. Model how asking questions helps readers find the main idea of a book. Ask: In a word or two, what is this book about? (This identifies the topic.) What is the most important idea about the topic? (This identifies the main idea.) What are some details that tell more about the main idea? As students read, have them think about what could be the main idea of the book and what details may support it.

GRAPHIC ORGANIZERS *Graphic organizers* are pictorial devices that help students view and construct relationships among concepts. Use an overhead projector to guide students through the completion of a main idea organizer. Then invite them to fill one out on their own during an independent reading period.

ADDITIONAL SKILL INSTRUCTION

GENERALIZE Remind students that they are often given ideas about several related things. To make a statement about all of them together is to *generalize* about them. This statement might tell how the things are mostly or completely alike in some way. Have students look for generalizations in the book. Clue words such as *most, many, usually, few, seldom, all,* and *generally* can signal generalizations.

Name _____

Main Idea

- The **main idea** is the most important idea about a paragraph, passage, article, or book.
- **Details** are pieces of information that support, or tell more about, the main idea.

Directions Read the following passage. What is the main idea of the paragraph? Write it in the box at the top. Then find three details that tell about the main idea. Write one detail in each smaller box.

> Antarctica is very windy and dry. Antarctica is so dry that scientists call it a desert. The small amount of snow that falls there never melts. It is moved around by the wind until it freezes into ice.

1.

2.

3.

4.

Vocabulary

Directions For each vocabulary word, write the letter of the definition that matches it.

Check the Words You Know
___cuddles ___flippers ___frozen ___hatch
___pecks ___preen ___snuggles

1. _____ cuddles   **a.** strikes at with the beak

2. _____ flippers   **b.** presses closely against, as for comfort

3. _____ frozen   **c.** to come out of an egg

4. _____ hatch   **d.** hugs closely

5. _____ pecks   **e.** flat body parts that are used for swimming

6. _____ preen   **f.** turned into ice

7. _____ snuggles   **g.** to clean and smooth feathers

Directions Write the vocabulary word or words that go best with each clue.

8. This word describes Antarctica. _____

9. Penguins use these to swim well. _____

10. A penguin chick does this to its eggshell. _____

11. This is another word for how a penguin chick is born. _____

Directions Write a short paragraph. Use at least three of the vocabulary words.

_____

_____

_____

_____

_____

_____

_____

Sarah's Choice

SUMMARY While playing with a neighborhood friend, Sarah makes a wrong decision by ignoring her mother's directions. Sarah picks a snack other than the one her mother had told her about, and she doesn't check to see if it's okay. This decision has consequences for her and her friend later in the day.

LESSON VOCABULARY

excitement	gardener
motioned	sadness
shivered	shocked
slammed	

INTRODUCE THE BOOK

INTRODUCE THE TITLE AND AUTHOR Discuss with students the title and the author of *Sarah's Choice*. Ask: What does it mean to make a choice? What must you think about before making one? How can you tell good choices from bad ones?

BUILD BACKGROUND Ask volunteers to talk about a time when they ignored instructions from a parent or teacher. What happened? What did they learn from the experience?

PREVIEW/USE ILLUSTRATIONS Have students preview the book by looking at the title and illustrations. How might the title tell what the pictures and story are about?

READ THE BOOK

SET PURPOSE Have students set a purpose for reading *Sarah's Choice*. Suggest that they think about a time when they, like the girl mentioned in the title, had to make choices in real-life situations. How did they make their choices, and what happened as a result? Were their choices good or bad? Why? Tell students they can ask the same questions about Sarah's choice in the story and seek answers in their reading.

STRATEGY SUPPORT: VISUALIZE Encourage students to use their own experience and knowledge as they visualize. Try to have students relate details in the book to details they recall from their own experience. Ask questions such as, "As you picture the inside of Sarah's house, how is it like other houses you have seen?"

COMPREHENSION QUESTIONS

PAGE 8 How is Sarah different from Julia when making decisions? Explain. *(Sarah does not ask her mother for permission when making decisions.)*

PAGE 10 What happened as a result of Sarah's choice? *(They couldn't bake the cake, which made Sarah feel sad.)*

PAGE 11 What do you think Sarah will do the next time she should ask permission to do something? *(She is likely to ask for it.)*

REVISIT THE BOOK

READER RESPONSE

1. Possible response: Sarah does not always follow other people's directions.
2. Responses will vary.
3. Possible response: 1. surprised 2. to have received an electric shock Sentences will vary.
4. Students should indicate how they would change their behavior to make a better choice in a specific situation.

EXTEND UNDERSTANDING Explore the element of theme with students by asking questions such as, "What does the author want readers to learn from reading this story?" Have them determine the story's "big idea," based on their responses, and explain how the events and characters support their findings.

RESPONSE OPTIONS

WRITING Ask students to write about the kinds of decisions that Sarah and Julia made in the story. Which choices were right? Which were wrong? Have them offer advice for both girls on what they should do in future situations where they may be tempted to ignore other people's directions.

WORD WORK *Alliteration* is when phrases or sentences contain several words with the same initial sounds. Provide a sample sentence, such as, "Sarah suddenly sprang sideways as the sprinkler sprayed her." Then challenge students to come up with other sentences that show alliteration.

SOCIAL STUDIES CONNECTION

Time For SOCIAL STUDIES

Discuss why it is important to follow rules and directions at home and in school. Identify situations where it would be dangerous to disobey rules, such as during a fire drill.

Skill Work

TEACH/REVIEW VOCABULARY

Have volunteers point out how this week's vocabulary words are used in the book. Then ask them how each word helped them better understand the story and its characters.

TARGET SKILL AND STRATEGY

CHARACTER Tell students that a *character* is a person who takes part in the events of a story. Ask them to identify the three main characters in the book. Then explain that the qualities or characteristics of a character are known as *character traits* and that they usually relate to his/her personality. While students are reading, have them identify the character traits of Sarah, Julia, and Sarah's mom based on clues and details in the story.

VISUALIZE *Visualizing* lets students create pictures in their minds by using their senses and prior knowledge. It helps them become so involved in a story that they feel they are part of it. A reader's mental images come not from just seeing, but also from smelling, touching, tasting, and hearing. Point out specific instances in the book that offer strong opportunities for visualizing. What does a warm summer day feel like? How might it feel to run through sprinklers? What might the lemonade left by Sarah's mom taste like?

ADDITIONAL SKILL INSTRUCTION

SEQUENCE The *sequence* of a story's events is the order in which events occur. Students should use sequence skills to keep track of which events happened first, next, and last for a correct understanding of books such as *Sarah's Choice*. Ask students how the story would change if the events were in a different order. Would it have the same meaning if Sarah and Julia ate the blueberries before Sarah's mom told them to just have lemonade?

ELL Show students how to make a simple sequencing diagram to follow the order of the events in the story.

Name _____

Character

- A **character** is a person who takes part in the events of a story.
- The qualities of a character are known as **character traits** and usually tell about his or her personality.

Directions How are Sarah and Julia alike? How are they different? Use the Venn Diagram below to compare the two characters.

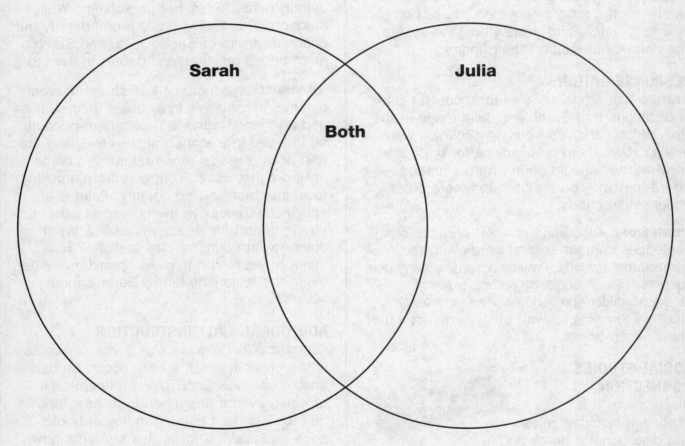

Name _____

Vocabulary

Directions Draw a line to match each vocabulary word with its definition.

Check the Words You Know

___excitement   ___gardener   ___motioned   ___sadness
___shivered   ___shocked   ___slammed

---

1. shivered   **a.** thrill

2. slammed   **b.** signaled

3. excitement   **c.** a person who works outdoors with plants

4. motioned   **d.** trembled

5. shocked   **e.** a feeling of unhappiness

6. gardener   **f.** to be surprised

7. sadness   **g.** closed with a bang

Directions Write the vocabulary word that completes each sentence.

8. I was _____ when I heard he was joining the circus.

9. The fact that we might never see each other again filled me with
   _____.

10. She _____ as she stepped out into the cold.

11. He stomped angrily out of the room and _____ the door
    behind him.

12. I wondered why the _____ planted the bushes so close
    to the house.

13. When our team won the big game, everyone at school shared the
    _____.

14. When the new girl walked into the lunchroom, I _____ for
    her to come over to our table.

Metal Detector Detective

SUMMARY A boy named Joe is bored until his grandmother teaches him how to use a metal detector. Joe has a chance to use the device to find a gold ring that was lost by his grandmother's neighbor. He decides that using the metal detector will be a fun way to stay busy during the summer.

LESSON VOCABULARY

collection	enormous
realize	scattered
shiny	strain

INTRODUCE THE BOOK

INTRODUCE THE TITLE AND AUTHOR Discuss with students the title and the author of *Metal Detector Detective*. Ask them to look at the cover illustration and identify the metal detector. For what purposes might the person use a metal detector? How can students tell?

BUILD BACKGROUND Have students discuss times when they or someone they know helped others by coming up with a creative solution to a problem. What was the solution and how did it solve the problem? How did everyone feel afterward?

PREVIEW/USE TEXT FEATURES Read aloud the title and have students glance through the illustrations. Ask students to predict what type of story they will read and what will happen in it based on these features.

READ THE BOOK

SET PURPOSE Have students set a purpose for reading *Metal Detector Detective* by asking them questions about the title. What do detectives do and what type of story might have a detective in it? What might a detective be seeking with a metal detector? Ask students to base their answers on previously read books and their own prior knowledge.

STRATEGY SUPPORT: MONITOR AND FIX UP Students need to monitor their comprehension while reading by sorting out and organizing thoughts and questions that come up. This strategy helps them fill in gaps in their understanding and determine the book's main idea. In small groups, ask students to share their thoughts about *Metal Detector Detective*. Then help organize these responses in a main idea chart or web.

COMPREHENSION QUESTIONS

PAGE 7 How did Ms. Choi lose her gold ring? *(It most likely slipped from her finger while she was working in her garden.)*

PAGE 9 What solution did Joe and Grandma come up with for finding Ms. Choi's ring? Why did it make sense? *(They decided to use the metal detector to find the ring because the ring was made of metal.)*

PAGE 11 What might Joe do with the metal detector later in the summer? *(Possible response: He might find coins for his coin collection or metal cans for recycling.)*

REVISIT THE BOOK

READER RESPONSE

1. Possible response: You can solve problems more easily if you think creatively and use the right tools.

2. Joe searches the flower beds, the bushes, and the ivy.

3. Possible responses: *colossal, gigantic, huge, massive, titanic, big*

4. Possible responses: They can find sharp objects on lawns before they can harm people. They can help police find evidence in crimes.

EXTEND UNDERSTANDING Tell students that a character is someone who takes part in the events of a story. Then, explain that character traits are the qualities or characteristics of a character. Create a character web based on a person from the book. Then invite students to identify the character's traits and explain their responses with examples. Record these responses on the web.

RESPONSE OPTIONS

WRITING How should Joe spread the word about his services as a metal detector detective? Ask students to write an advertisement that promotes his services.

WORD WORK Provide students with magazines and newspapers and ask them to cut out pictures that show the meanings of the lesson vocabulary words. For example, an image of an elephant may represent the word "enormous." Have students paste their pictures on a separate sheet of paper and, under each image, write the corresponding word. Invite volunteers to share their work.

SCIENCE CONNECTION

TIME FOR Science

Remind students that a metal detector was used to search for a lost metal object in the story. Have students come up with other examples of how specific tools and devices are designed to solve specific problems.

Skill Work

TEACH/REVIEW VOCABULARY

Have volunteers define the vocabulary words and use them in sentences to help classmates improve their understanding of them.

ELL In pairs, have students make up a riddle game using vocabulary words. Suggest an example such as "I have a penny and it is very _____."

TARGET SKILL AND STRATEGY

MAIN IDEA Explain to students that the *main idea* in fiction explains what the story is about and identifies its most important ideas. Ask students to tell what the book is about in their own words and to provide reasons to support their answers.

MONITOR AND FIX UP When students *monitor* comprehension they know when they understand what they read and when they do not. There are strategies to restore their understanding when problems arise, such as summarizing facts and details to clarify and organize ideas. Tell students to use this strategy when they are unsure of meaning. Encourage them to write down these facts and details in a main idea chart.

ADDITIONAL SKILL INSTRUCTION

REALISM AND FANTASY Tell students that a *realistic* story tells about something that could happen, and a *fantasy* is a story about something that could not happen. Ask students to identify specific elements within *Metal Detector Detective* that indicate which type of story it is. Then have them point out previously read books that exemplify the other type of story and explain why.

Main Idea

- The **main idea** is the most important idea about a paragraph, passage, or article.
- **Details** are small pieces of information that tell more about the main idea.

Directions Read the following passage. What is the main idea of the paragraph? Write it in the box on the left. Then find three details that tell about the main idea. Write them in the boxes on the right.

> Using a metal detector can be a fun hobby. But there are rules you must follow before using a metal detector. Metal detectors are not allowed on National Park Service lands. There are also many places, such as public schools, churches, and private lands, where you must ask permission before you use a metal detector. If you are not sure of whether you can use a metal detector, just ask!

Main Idea

1.

Detail

2.

Detail

3.

Detail

4.

© Pearson Education 3

Vocabulary

Directions Draw a line to connect each vocabulary word with the correct description.

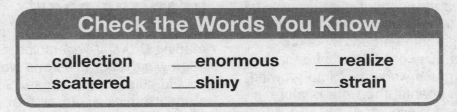

Check the Words You Know

___collection   ___enormous   ___realize
___scattered   ___shiny   ___strain

1. collection   a. sprinkled

2. enormous   b. giant

3. realize   c. glossy

4. scattered   d. struggle

5. shiny   e. group

6. strain   f. understand

Directions Write the vocabulary word that completes each clue.

7. This word describes the size of something.

_____

8. When you try hard, you do this.

_____

9. If you sprinkle seeds over a flower bed, you might describe the seeds this way.

_____

10. You often use this word to describe a new car.

_____

11. People organize seashells, stamps, dolls, and baseball cards into one of these.

_____

Growing Vegetables

SUMMARY This is a story about a group of kids working together for a common goal: planting and growing a vegetable garden. By taking readers through a busy day in the garden, the story shows how much work goes into growing a garden and how sharing the work is more fun and productive for everyone.

LESSON VOCABULARY

bottom	cheated	clever
crops	lazy	partners
wealth		

INTRODUCE THE BOOK

INTRODUCE THE TITLE AND AUTHOR Discuss with students the title and the author of *Growing Vegetables*. Point out the science content triangle on the cover and ask students how they think this may relate to the selection's title and content.

BUILD BACKGROUND Ask students if they have ever grown plants. Discuss what kind of plants they grew and how they cared for them. If students are interested, begin a discussion about different kinds of gardens, such as herb gardens or flower gardens, or about plants that grow in water or grow without soil.

PREVIEW/USE TEXT FEATURES As students preview the book, point out that illustrations can often help them when they encounter unfamiliar words, terms, or ideas. Direct their attention to page 8, where students will see a drawing of Alex's plant. The illustration helps students figure out what the words *bean plant* mean. Go through the rest of the illustrations with students and see if the drawings relate to any of the words in the text in the same way.

READ THE BOOK

SET PURPOSE Have students set a purpose for reading *Growing Vegetables*. Students' interest in growing vegetables and working together should guide this purpose. Suggest that students think about all that goes into growing the vegetables that they eat at home or see in the supermarket or at farm stands.

STRATEGY SUPPORT: PREDICT As students read about how vegetables grow, *predicting* gives them a chance to use what they already know and to imagine what is going to happen next in the story.

COMPREHENSION QUESTIONS

PAGE 3 Why does the Garden Bunch want to work together to plant a garden? *(They are friends who love to dig in the dirt.)*

PAGE 4 Why did the Garden Bunch plant their garden in a sunny spot? *(Vegetables need lots of sunlight to grow.)*

PAGE 7 Can you predict what will happen if Miranda forgets to water the carrots again? *(The carrots will wilt even more.)*

PAGE 10 Using clues in the text, explain what *harvest* means. *(It means to pick or gather.)*

REVIST THE BOOK

READER RESPONSE

1. Possible response: to inform readers about growing vegetables

2. Possible response: They may plant a new garden. The story says that the kids planted a garden last summer. This summer they grew new plants.

3. Possible response: *busy, lively*

4. Possible response: The plants were planted in rows; the vegetables were planted in separate areas; markers identified each crop.

EXTEND UNDERSTANDING Explain to students that identifying details and facts can help them understand what is important in a story. Discuss with students the facts they learned about growing things from this story. Ask them to write details about how to grow each plant mentioned in the story.

RESPONSE OPTIONS

WRITING Instruct students to look at the illustration of the Garden Bunch's vegetable stand on page 12. Ask them to write a short radio commercial for the stand.

WORD WORK Discuss with students how words like *clever* and *lazy* are adjectives, or descriptive words. Write on the board other adjectives that students know. Then hand out old magazines and ask students to cut out pictures and to write adjectives that describe them. Post pictures in the classroom.

SCIENCE CONNECTION

TIME FOR Science

Students can learn more about measuring by planting a fast-growing plant, such as a sunflower, in the classroom. Every week, ask students to measure the height of the flower as it grows. Suggest that students also track the growth on a weekly chart posted in the classroom.

Skill Work

TEACH/REVIEW VOCABULARY

To reinforce the meaning of the words, ask volunteers to think of a synonym for each word, such as *smart* for *clever*. Then have them think of an antonym for each word.

ELL Ask students to draw pictures that describe each vocabulary word and to write sentences about them.

TARGET SKILL AND STRATEGY

AUTHOR'S PURPOSE Remind students that every author has a *purpose,* or reason, for writing a story. An author may want to entertain, inform, or persuade. Ask students why they think this author wrote this story. Discuss with students what they imagine the author might want them to know about gardening.

PREDICT Remind students that *predicting* is when you guess what is going to happen next in a story based on what has already happened. As students read, remind them to note events that may help them guess what is going to happen next. As students read, suggest that they determine if their predictions were correct. Remind students that predicting is a great way to make sure they understand a story.

ADDITIONAL SKILL INSTRUCTION

GENERALIZE Remind students that a *generalization* is when you recognize similarities and differences about things in a story and come to some conclusion. Clue words such as *all, many, most,* or *never* can help students form generalizations. As students read, have them note any clue words. Ask students if they see common elements in what each gardener does. Suggest that these common elements allow them to make some generalizations about how to garden.

Author's Purpose

- The **author's purpose** is the reason or reasons the author has for writing.
- An author may have one or more reasons for writing. To *inform, persuade, entertain,* or *express* are common reasons.

Directions Answer the questions.

1. Why do you think the author wrote about the time Miranda forgot to water the plants?

_____

_____

_____

2. Why do you think the author told about the special job each person had?

_____

_____

_____

3. Why do you think the author wrote a book about growing vegetables?

_____

_____

_____

4. What do you think the author wanted you to learn about plants?

_____

_____

_____

5. What do you think the author wanted you to learn about working together?

_____

_____

_____

Vocabulary

Directions Circle the letter of the correct definition below each vocabulary word.

Check the Words You Know

___bottom	___cheated	___clever	___crops
___lazy	___partners	___wealth	

1. lazy
   a. quick   b. not wanting to do any work   c. simple to do

2. crops
   a. big hairy dogs   b. clothing   c. plants or fruits

3. partners
   a. wooden fences   b. people who work together   c. enemies

4. cheated
   a. not playing fairly   b. dressed for dinner   c. destroyed

5. clever
   a. hungry   b. silly   c. smart

6. wealth
   a. dirt   b. money   c. talent

7. bottom
   a. lowest part   b. highest part   c. middle

Directions Unscramble the letters to form a vocabulary word.

8. TAEEHCD _____

9. CREVEL _____

10. TOMBOT _____

11. PRCOS _____

12. PTNSERAR _____

13. ZALY _____

14. HTWEAL _____

Colonial New England

SUMMARY The author describes how early colonists met basic needs of food, clothing, and shelter without the existence of super-markets, shopping malls, and ready-made houses. The work habits and education of children reveal the demands of life back then.

LESSON VOCABULARY
   barrels
   cellar
   clearing
   peg
   spoil
   steep

INTRODUCE THE BOOK

INTRODUCE THE TITLE AND AUTHOR Discuss with students the title and the author of *Colonial New England*. Have them share what they already know about colonial times and New England. Based on their responses, talk about what information they think this book will provide.

BUILD BACKGROUND Ask students to discuss how they would feel if they did not have modern conveniences such as refrigerators, supermarkets, ready-to-wear clothing, and video games. What could they do to meet their needs?

PREVIEW/USE TEXT FEATURES Tell students to look at the pictures and read the captions while flipping through the book. Ask them to share any impressions they may have about colonial life based on these words and images.

READ THE BOOK

SET PURPOSE Have students set a purpose for reading *Colonial New England*. Ask them how they think people survived without today's modern conveniences. Their curiosity should guide their purpose.

STRATEGY SUPPORT: ASK QUESTIONS Remind students that asking questions involves knowing how to ask good questions about important text information. Use recip-rocal teaching to create a dialogue where students and you take turns asking ques-tions about the text. Read a section of text together. Model how to ask important ques-tions about it, and call on students to answer the questions. Guide them as they develop their own questions (to be answered by class-mates), and encourage them to take over more and more of the activity until they can work independently.

COMPREHENSION QUESTIONS

PAGE 3 Why was colonial America called New England by settlers? *(Most settlers came to America from England, so their new home was like a "new" England.)*

PAGE 4 Was it easy for colonists to get clothing to wear? Why or why not? *(No. They had to make almost everything themselves. They made yarn from sheep's wool and wove it into cloth.)*

PAGES 8–9 How were colonists' choices and sources of food similar and different from those of people today? *(Like modern people, they ate vegetables, cornbread, bacon, ham, eggs, and milk. Unlike modern people, they did not have supermarkets. Instead, they raised their food themselves.)*

PAGE 9 Why was food salted, smoked, dried, and stored in cool places? *(These methods prevented food from spoiling during a time when there were no refrigerators.)*

REVISIT THE BOOK

READER RESPONSE

1. Responses will vary.
2. Responses will vary but may include questions about playtime, chores, learning to read and write, and family life.
3. *Clearing* means to remove things such as trees and rocks to create bare ground where seeds can be planted; so that they can build and plant things
4. Responses will vary, but will probably include mudwalls, small size, furniture, and dirt floor.

EXTEND UNDERSTANDING Invite students to look at the photographs and illustrations. Discuss the similarities and differences between the aspects of colonial life shown in the images and their modern-day counterparts.

RESPONSE OPTIONS

WRITING Ask students to pretend they are children in colonial New England. Have them write a journal entry about a typical day in their lives.

WORD WORK Draw simple pictures to represent each vocabulary word. Then create rebus sentences. Have students translate each sentence by writing the correct vocabulary words.

ELL Help students sort words related to colonial New England by creating categories such as food, clothing, and homes.

SOCIAL STUDIES CONNECTION

Provide reference materials that will help students learn more about different roles that colonists played in their communities. Then ask students to work in pairs, with one person playing the part of interviewer and the other playing a colonist with a specific job. After asking questions about work and writing down responses, students may switch roles and repeat the activity.

Time For SOCIAL STUDIES

Skill Work

TEACH/REVIEW VOCABULARY

Before reading, introduce the lesson vocabulary words by asking students if they recognize any of them. Have volunteers use the words in sentences based on real-life experiences to help others better understand meaning.

TARGET SKILL AND STRATEGY

DRAW CONCLUSIONS Tell students that a *conclusion* is a decision you reach after you think about what you have read. When students use details to make reasonable decisions about characters or events, they are drawing conclusions. Model how to draw conclusions by using diagrams or a chart with spaces to write facts from the book, what one already knows, and the conclusions that result. Then have students practice sharing facts and prior knowledge about the topic while making conclusions. Write down their responses in the modeled diagram.

ASK QUESTIONS This strategy involves asking good *questions* about important text information. Good questions often start with a question word such as *who, what, when, where, why,* or *how.* They are about important details in the story and are usually answered by information in the story. Ask students to write down questions they have while reading about Colonial New England. Students who ask questions and find answers during their reading are better able to draw conclusions.

ADDITIONAL SKILL INSTRUCTION

COMPARE AND CONTRAST Tell students that to *compare* is to identify how two or more things are alike, and to *contrast* is to identify how they are different. Ask students to compare and contrast aspects of life in colonial New England and modern life in their area. Suggest that they use a Venn Diagram to chart similarities and differences.

Draw Conclusions

- **Drawing conclusions** means using what you already know and what you read to make reasonable decisions about characters or events.

Directions Read the following passage. Then fill in the charts with facts from the passage and things you know that are related to the facts. Finally, write conclusions based on the facts and what you know.

There are no shopping malls in 1650. New England colonists have to make almost everything themselves. When they need clothes, they make yarn from sheep's wool. Then they weave the yarn into wool cloth. Finally, they sew the cloth into clothing.

Men and boys in colonial New England wear shirts with long sleeves. Their pants, called breeches, go to their knees. They wear long stockings.

Girls dress like their mothers. They wear long wool dresses and aprons. Outdoors and indoors, they wear caps called coifs.

1.

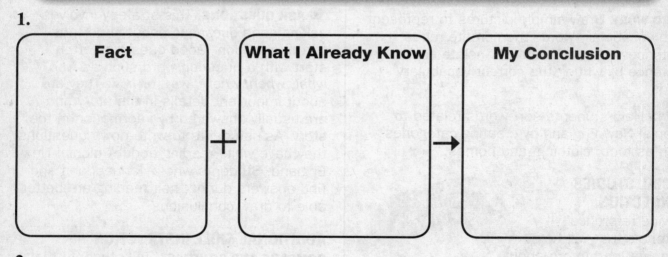

Fact		What I Already Know		My Conclusion
	+		→	

2.

Fact		What I Already Know		My Conclusion
	+		→	

Name _____

Vocabulary

Directions Write the word that best completes each sentence.

> ## Check the Words You Know
>
> ___barrels   ___cellar   ___clearing
>
> ___peg   ___spoil   ___steep

1. Your food will _____ unless you put it in the refrigerator.

2. My coat is hanging from a _____ on the wall.

3. The mountain was hard to climb because it was very _____.

4. The man sells pickles in large _____ at the market.

5. The underground _____ is a good place to store things.

6. There is a _____ in the middle of the forest where you can have a picnic.

Directions Write a paragraph about life in colonial New England. Use at least four vocabulary words.

_____

_____

_____

_____

_____

_____

_____

_____

_____

Gardening with Grandpa

SUMMARY In this story, a grandfather shows his twin granddaughters how to garden. Readers learn about the planting and caring for a garden, particularly how to grow both seeds and bulbs.

LESSON VOCABULARY

beauty	blooming
bulbs	doze
humor	recognizing
showers	sprouting

INTRODUCE THE BOOK

INTRODUCE THE TITLE AND AUTHOR Discuss with students the title and the author of *Gardening with Grandpa*. Point out the word "Science" in the triangle on the cover and ask students how they imagine this story might have to do with science. Ask students what the cover illustration makes them think the story might be about.

BUILD BACKGROUND Ask students if they have ever seen seeds and bulbs and what they looked like. Then ask students if they have ever planted seeds or bulbs and what steps they had to take to ensure the seeds or bulbs would grow.

PREVIEW/USE TEXT FEATURES Ask students to look at the illustrations in the story and then lead them to share what comes to mind. Direct students' attention to the picture on page 8 and to the words "seeds by mail" in the drawing. Guide them to explain how the illustration gives them more information about the story. Repeat this process with the illustration on page 10.

READ THE BOOK

SET PURPOSE Have students set a purpose for reading *Gardening with Grandpa*. Students' curiosity about growing things or their interests in grandparents should guide this purpose.

STRATEGY SUPPORT: TEXT STRUCTURE As students read *Gardening with Grandpa*, encourage them to fill out their graphic organizer, listing the chain of events in the story. Remind students that not all events are important and need to be listed.

COMPREHENSION QUESTIONS

PAGE 5 What did Gramps tell the girls would happen if they planted a bulb now? *(Tulips would bloom in the spring.)*

PAGE 6 What was the sequence for growing things in the garden? *(First push bulbs in the dirt. Then wait until spring when the bulbs will sprout.)*

PAGE 9 Why is a Venus Flytrap a good plant for a garden? *(It catches insects.)*

PAGE 10 What would you need for a backyard or garden makeover? *(Possible response: I would need a new hoe, a rake, gloves, and bulbs.)*

REVISIT THE BOOK

READER RESPONSE

1. They were bored. They planted seeds and bulbs in Gramps's garden and became interested.
2. Possible response: At the beginning, they were making over each other's hair. At the end, they were gardeners.
3. Sentences will vary.
4. Responses will vary.

EXTEND UNDERSTANDING Remind students that a character is the person who does the action in a story. Ask students to identify the characters in the story and make character maps, listing all the details they know about the characters.

RESPONSE OPTIONS

WRITING Ask students to imagine they are Judy and May and that it is a year later. Have them write postcards to their friends describing Gramps' garden and their work in it. Suggest students use lots of detail about what kind of plants are in the garden now.

SCIENCE CONNECTION

TIME FOR Science

Have students grow bean plants in the class from seeds planted in paper cups. Make a chart so students can keep track of the plant growth, watering, amount of sunlight, and any other details related to nurturing the plant.

Skill Work

TEACH/REVIEW VOCABULARY

Review vocabulary words with students. Then lead a game of hangman with students using the words. As students complete a word, have them use it in a sentence you write on the board.

TARGET SKILL AND STRATEGY

CAUSE AND EFFECT Remind students that *cause* is why something happened and *effect* is what happened. Clue words like *because*, *so* and *since* can help students connect causes and effects. After reading, write five events that happened in the story in a column on the chalkboard. Ask students to recall why the events happened. Write their answers in a second column. Prompt students to identify which column should be labeled "causes" and which column should be labeled "effects."

ELL After teaching cause and effect, ask students to make sentences using a cause, a clue word, and the effect. If students need more support, supply the causes, effects, and clue words for them.

TEXT STRUCTURE Remind students that *text structure* is the way a story is organized and that this story tells the events in the order in which they happened, or in sequence. Prompt students to map out the story's chain of events in a graphic organizer during or after reading. Point out that recognizing a story's structure can help students identify cause-and-effect relationships.

ADDITIONAL SKILL INSTRUCTION

GENERALIZE Remind students that a *generalization* is a broad statement or rule that applies to many examples and often uses clue words like *all, none, most, many, always, in general, never, usually,* and *few.* Lead students to identify generalizations about gardening as they read and to support these generalizations with details from the story.

Name _____

Cause and Effect

- An **effect** is something that happens.
- A **cause** is why it happened.

Directions Use the story *Gardening with Grandpa* to match each cause with an effect. Write the letter of the effect next to its cause. Each cause has only one effect.

Causes	Effects
1. The girls were bored. ____	**a.** This allows the small green plant to catch insects.
2. Gramps said his garden needed a makeover. ____	**b.** The girls needed to choose plants that love the sun.
3. It is fall now. ____	**c.** Judy and May followed Gramps to the garden.
4. The girls planted bulbs in the fall. ____	**d.** Nothing is growing in Gramps's garden.
5. The spring showers come. ____	**e.** The garden grew.
6. A Venus Flytrap has trigger hairs that act like jaws. ____	**f.** Now they could call themselves gardeners.
7. The garden got watered. ____	**g.** Tulips will bloom in the spring.
8. Gramps's garden is in a sunny spot. ____	**h.** The girls were thirsty when they were finished.
9. The girls gave the garden a makeover. ____	**i.** They began to doze off.
10. The girls worked hard in the hot sun. ____	**j.** Then the bulbs will start sprouting.

Name _____

Vocabulary

Directions For each word or phrase below, write the vocabulary word that has the same meaning. Use each word only once.

Check the Words You Know

___beauty	___blooming	___bulbs	___doze
___humor	___recognizing	___showers	___sprouting

---

1. growing _____

2. a funny aspect of something _____

3. flowering _____

4. knowing _____

5. light rains _____

6. onion-like plant starters _____

7. something that is pretty _____

8. to sleep _____

Directions Complete the sentences using the vocabulary words.

9. That red rose is a real _____.

10. There may be _____.

11. Tulips are grown from _____, not seeds.

12. The girls were so tired after helping Gramps that they began to

_____.

13. The _____ flowers show that spring is really here.

14. Gramps made the girls laugh because he has such a good sense of

_____.

15. _____ that the girls loved flowers, Grandpa let
    them pick the seeds.

The Elk Hunters

SUMMARY This nonfiction book introduces students to the Snohomish people and tells how they created their own myth for how and why the Big Dipper is in the sky. The book invites students to think about why and how stories are created and passed down. The book helps students learn how to summarize and how to identify the author's purpose in writing the story.

LESSON VOCABULARY

antlers	imagined
language	narrator
overhead	poke

INTRODUCE THE BOOK

INTRODUCE THE TITLE AND AUTHOR Discuss with students the title and the author of *The Elk Hunter*. Based on the title, ask students what kind of information they think this book will provide. Ask them what they imagine the people on the cover are doing and why they might be looking at the stars. Encourage them to support their answer with clues in the illustrations.

BUILD BACKGROUND Discuss with students what they know about the constellations and the stars. Ask students if they have ever star-gazed, seen a shooting star, or looked through a telescope. Ask: What do you think about when you look at a star or wish upon it?

PREVIEW/USE TEXT FEATURES Invite students to take a picture walk through the illustrations. Ask how the illustrations give clues to the meaning of the story. Discuss with students which illustrations seem realistic and which seem like fantasy, and why.

READ THE BOOK

SET PURPOSE Have students set a purpose for reading *The Elk Hunter*. Their curiosity about the stars, myths, and Native American culture should guide this purpose. Suggest that as students read, they take notes to summarize the story and to provide answers for any questions they might have about the stars, myths, or Native American culture.

STRATEGY SUPPORT: SUMMARIZE Remind students that to summarize means to boil down a story to its main ideas. Ask students to take notes as they read, including the main points of the story and supporting ideas.

COMPREHENSION QUESTIONS

PAGE 3 Summarize why the elk are important to the Snohomish. *(They give meat for food, their skin is used for clothing, and tools, weapons and art are made from their antlers.)*

PAGE 6 Can you imagine a reason why the Creator had not made the sky high enough? *(Possible responses: The Creator was busy and forgot; the Creator wanted the people to work together to push the sky up.)*

PAGE 9 What was the author's purpose in writing about why the elk were important? *(To explain why the Snohomish would name a constellation after them.)*

PAGE 11 How does this story prove that it's important to work together? *(That's how the Snohomish were able to lift the sky.)*

REVISIT THE BOOK

READER RESPONSE

1. Possible response: The author wanted to explain how the Snohomish people thought the Big Dipper was placed in the sky.

2. Responses will vary.

3. Possible responses: I could look at the other words around it. I could look it up in a dictionary.

4. Possible response: Instead of the hunters chasing elk, they would probably be chasing another animal.

EXTEND UNDERSTANDING Remind students that *sequence* is the order in which story events happen. Have students write the sequence of events in *The Elk Hunters.* Ask: How might the story be different if any of the events were shuffled around? Invite students to change the events and write a new myth.

RESPONSE OPTIONS

WRITING Introduce students to a variety of different myths and then suggest that they write their own myth about the Little Dipper. Have students present their myths to the class.

SCIENCE CONNECTIONS

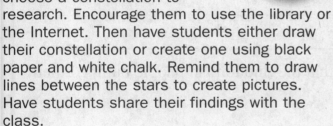

Provide or have students choose a constellation to research. Encourage them to use the library or the Internet. Then have students either draw their constellation or create one using black paper and white chalk. Remind them to draw lines between the stars to create pictures. Have students share their findings with the class.

Skill Work

TEACH/REVIEW VOCABULARY

To reinforce the contextual meaning of *overhead* on page 4, discuss with students how the phrase "in the night sky" helps to guess the meaning of *overhead*. Do this with the other vocabulary words in the story.

TARGET SKILL AND STRATEGY

AUTHOR'S PURPOSE Remind students that the *author's purpose* is the reason why a writer wrote a particular story. An author's purpose can be to entertain, to convince, to express, or to give information. Ask: Why might an author write a story called *The Elk Hunters*? Remind students that as they read, they can take notes which might help them determine the author's purpose.

SUMMARIZE Remind students that *summarizing* is boiling down a story to its main points. Once you identify the main points, you can find details that support that point. To give students practice in the skill, ask them to summarize a familiar story like *The Three Little Pigs*. Remind students that summarizing a story can also help them determine the author's purpose.

ELL Ask students to summarize what they did yesterday. Have them provide one main idea and three supporting details.

ADDITIONAL SKILL INSTRUCTION

THEME Without using the word *theme,* remind students that every story has one big idea or lesson. Discuss with students the themes of familiar stories like *The Ant and the Grasshopper. (prepare for the future)* Ask students how that big idea teaches them a lesson.

Author's Purpose

- The **author's purpose** is the reason or reasons why an author writes, such as *to inform, to persuade, to express* or *to entertain.*
- An author may have one or more reasons for writing.

Directions Reread *The Elk Hunters*. Then answer the questions below.

1. Why do you think the author of The Elk Hunter had all the people working together to push up the sky?

_____

_____

2. Name two details that the author gave about the Snohomish people that tell you something about their lives.

_____

_____

3. Why do you think the author wrote that the Snohomish people named a part of a constellation after the elk?

_____

_____

4. What was the author's purpose in writing that the Snohomish people bumped their heads on the stars?

_____

_____

5. Why do you think the author wrote that the people needed a word as a signal to mean "lift up the sky"?

_____

_____

Vocabulary

Directions Circle the best definition for each word below. Then use the word in a sentence.

> ## Check the Words You Know
>
> ___antlers   ___imagined   ___language
> ___narrator   ___overheard   ___poke

1. Antlers

   a. the horns on an animal's head

   b. the sharp hoofs of an animal

2. _____

_____

3. Imagined

   a. laughed very loudly

   b. to form a mental image

4. _____

_____

5. Language

   a. the words people use to communicate

   b. the way people sing

6. _____

_____

7. Overheard

   a. to listen intently

   b. to hear without the speaker's knowledge

8. _____

_____

Paws and Claws: Learn About Animal Tracks

SUMMARY This book highlights how we can learn to identify animals by their tracks. Students will learn about the kinds of information that can be found by studying the tracks of cats, dogs, birds, and bears.

LESSON VOCABULARY

blade	budding
dew	fireflies
flutter	hawkmoth
notepad	patch

INTRODUCE THE BOOK

INTRODUCE THE TITLE AND AUTHOR Discuss with students the title and the author of *Paws and Claws: Learn About Animal Tracks*. Ask: Based on the cover photograph and the title, what do you think the book might be about? Direct students' attention to the "Science" triangle on the cover and ask them how they imagine tracking animals might be scientific.

BUILD BACKGROUND Ask students if they have ever compared the size and shape of their footprints with those of other people. Discuss with students the kinds of tracks they have noticed and where they saw them.

PREVIEW/USE TEXT FEATURES Have students look at the captions for the animal tracks in this reader. Ask: If the tracks had not been captioned, would you have been able to tell what kind of animal made them? Direct students' attention to the chart on page 6. Discuss how this graphic organizer shows how animals walk and what kinds of tracks they leave.

READ THE BOOK

SET PURPOSE Have students set a purpose for reading *Paws and Claws: Learn About Animal Tracks*. Students' interest and curiosity in animals and their tracks should guide this purpose.

STRATEGY SUPPORT: ASK QUESTIONS As they read, have students fill in the answers to the questions they posed earlier in their graphic organizer. When they finish reading, ask students if they have more questions. Suggest they write these new questions and research the answers.

COMPREHENSION QUESTIONS

PAGE 5 What conclusions can you make about the easiest places to find animal tracks? *(where the ground is soft or wet)*

PAGE 7 Do animals have to have feet to make tracks? Support your answer. *(No. A snake leaves a trail with the motion of its body.)*

PAGES 8–9 What conclusions can you make about claws and tracks? *(Except for cats, you can often identify animals by the claw marks in their tracks.)*

REVISIT THE BOOK

READER RESPONSE

1. It must be a dog because its claw marks are showing. Cats pull in their claws when walking or running.
2. Answers will vary.
3. Responses will vary.
4. Possible response: It grouped tracks into categories.

EXTEND UNDERSTANDING Direct students' attention to the selection's subheads and discuss how they help readers understand the text and how it is organized. Ask: Which subheads are funny? (*Possible responses: Not so fast!* and *It's for the birds!*) Which show excitement? (*Possible response: Tracks make patterns!*) Which are straightforward? (*Possible response: Who tracks animals? Not all tracks look the same.*) Invite students to create subheads of their own.

RESPONSE OPTIONS

WRITING Invite students to choose an animal in the reader and to imagine what it was doing when its tracks were discovered. Have students imagine they are the animal, and ask them to write about making tracks. Invite volunteers to share their essays with the class.

SCIENCE CONNECTION

TIME FOR Science

Suggest students research the tracks of an animal not included in the selection. Ask students to draw the tracks on a piece of paper without labeling them. Challenge other students to guess what animal made the tracks. Post drawings around the room.

Skill Work

TEACH/REVIEW VOCABULARY

Review vocabulary words with students. Then write their meanings on flash cards and challenge students to tell you the vocabulary word that matches each meaning.

ELL After reviewing vocabulary words with students, make two sets of index cards: one with the words and the other with their definitions. Have students match each word to the right definition.

TARGET SKILL AND STRATEGY

DRAW CONCLUSIONS Remind students that *drawing conclusions* means making a sensible decision after thinking about facts and details. To give students practice, give them a list of three sentences about cats (*Cats know when it's dinnertime, Cats recognize their owners, Cats can be trained to do tricks*) and ask students to draw a conclusion about cats based on this information. (*Conclusion: Cats are smart.*)

ASK QUESTIONS Remind students that *asking questions* can help them better understand their reading. Ask students what questions they have about tracking animals. Have them write their questions in a graphic organizer that they can use as they read. Remind students that asking questions can also help them come to conclusions about what they are reading.

ADDITIONAL SKILL INSTRUCTION

AUTHOR'S PURPOSE Remind students that *author's purpose* is the reason an author writes a selection, such as to inform, to entertain, to persuade, or to express feelings. Ask students what they imagine this author wants them to know about animal tracks, and discuss how skimming through the reader can help them determine this.

Draw Conclusions

- When you **draw a conclusion**, you figure out something by using clues and what you know.
- Remember that drawing conclusions means thinking about facts and details and then making a decision that makes sense.

Directions Read the following sentences. Mark the correct conclusion for each sentence.

1. A crow track has three marks, while a snake track looks like a long winding line.

   ___ Tracks make patterns.

   ___ Snake tracks are bigger than crow tracks.

2. Cat tracks show four toes. Dog tracks and rodent tracks also show four toes.

   ___ Tracks are easier to see in damp ground.

   ___ Many animal tracks show four toes.

3. Fireflies flutter and bees fly. Neither fireflies nor bees walk much on the ground.

   ___ Fireflies and bees don't leave tracks.

   ___ Fireflies and bees are annoying insects.

Directions Read each sentence below. Draw a conclusion and write a sentence about it.

4. Harry was crying.

   _____

   _____

5. Annie hid behind her mother when she saw the big dog.

   _____

   _____

© Pearson Education 3

Name _____

Vocabulary

Directions Complete each sentence with a word from the box.

Check the Words You Know

___blade	___budding	___dew	___fireflies
___flutter	___hawkmoth	___notepad	___patch

1. Get out your _____ and draw some animal tracks.

2. Fireflies _____.

3. Doesn't the grass look pretty with the _____ sparkling on it?

4. The roses are _____.

5. There was no wind at all, not even a _____.

6. That _____ of grass looks like a perfect place to have our picnic.

7. _____ look like tiny lights.

8. The _____ is a kind of insect.

Directions Select three vocabulary words and use each in a sentence.

9. _____

_____

10. _____

_____

11. _____

_____

Rescuing Stranded Whales

SUMMARY This book introduces the basic concepts surrounding beached, or stranded, whales. Steps of a rescue are described, including how whales are returned to the sea.

LESSON VOCABULARY

anxiously	bay	blizzard
channel	chip	melody
supplies	surrounded	symphony

INTRODUCE THE BOOK

INTRODUCE THE TITLE AND AUTHOR Discuss with students the title and the author of *Rescuing Stranded Whales*. Ask students what they know about whales or any animals in trouble.

BUILD BACKGROUND Most students have not seen a beached whale, but many know about this situation from films or television. Tell students that they will read about keeping a whale alive during its rescue. As they read, suggest that students watch for the first actions of a rescue and determine why they are important to the whale's safety.

PREVIEW/USE TEXT FEATURES Tell students to look at the photographs, map, and journal time line. Ask: What do you notice in the photographs about the people watching the rescue? Draw attention to the journal time line on pages 10–11, and ask students to predict why a whale rescue follows a schedule.

ELL Invite students to share any experiences they may have had with animal rescue or a close call they have had with a sick or injured animal.

READ THE BOOK

SET PURPOSE Most students will be interested in reading this book so that they can learn why whales beach and how to help a beached whale.

STRATEGY SUPPORT: ANSWER QUESTIONS Ask students to see what questions the author raises and how further reading helps you answer them. After reading, encourage students to think about what they read and to go back to the text for answers. As they begin to formulate a generalization, these questions and answers will help them assess the importance of what they read.

COMPREHENSION QUESTIONS

PAGE 4 Why is it important to immediately cool a beached whale? *(Its body temperature can become very high.)*

PAGE 7 Why don't scientists know what causes a whale to strand? *(Many possible causes make it difficult to pin down one.)*

PAGES 8–11 What happened when three pilot whales beached themselves in Massachusetts? *(Scientists decided to take the whales to the aquarium, where they healed and adjusted to aquarium life until they were ready to be returned to the sea.)*

PAGE 11 Why do scientists find a pod of whales before lowering a whale into the water? *(Calves need to be with other whales for survival.)*

REVISIT THE BOOK

READER RESPONSE

1. Possible response: Like whales, dolphins need to be directed into deep water.
2. Responses will vary.
3. Possible response: gathered around or encircled
4. three hours

EXTEND UNDERSTANDING Ask: Did photographs draw you into this book more quickly than illustrations would have? How is a rescue more meaningful if you can see real people in action? (Possible response: The reader can often identify more with what's going on in the text.)

RESPONSE OPTIONS

WRITING Tell students to pretend they are scientists who specialize in whales. Ask them to write about how they would handle a rescue. Encourage them visit the library and browse the Internet. Their research should help them include facts about why the whale stranded and what the effects of the rescue might be on the whale.

SOCIAL STUDIES CONNECTION

Time For SOCIAL STUDIES

Suggest that students have a "Humans Care for Animals" day. Volunteers can bring in photos or drawings of the many ways humans can help animals. Make captions for each photo or drawing, and display them in the classroom.

Skill Work

TEACH/REVIEW VOCABULARY

Ask students why this book about whale rescue features words such as *anxiously*, *melody*, and *symphony*. The title shows that a whale is in trouble, which is a reason to be anxious; whales are known to sing playful or mournful melodies. Ask students to look at the other vocabulary words and predict their use in a book about rescuing a whale. Use a map to deal with the geographical or weather-related words.

TARGET SKILL AND STRATEGY

GENERALIZE After reading about a typical whale rescue scene, students should have a general idea of what is involved in helping a stranded whale. Remind students that a *generalization* is a broad statement or rule that applies to many examples. A good place to practice generalizing may be to read over the time line and make statements about the ways people help keep whales alive and safe while they return them to the sea. (Scientists use ships to carry the whales back to pods in deep waters and then finally lower them into the water from special cages.)

ANSWER QUESTIONS To help themselves generalize, students should ask themselves questions about the rescue as they read. Help them organize their answers into logical generalizations.

ADDITIONAL SKILL INSTRUCTION

SEQUENCE Remind students that understanding sequence, the order of events, can help them keep track of what is going on in the text. In this case, a sequence is graphically displayed in the journal time line on pages 10–11. Students may also read about the events from page 8 on and put them in order, leading up to the day's events when the whales were returned to sea.

Name _____

Generalize

- When authors present one statement about many ideas or people, they **generalize**.
- A generalization is a kind of conclusion.

Directions Choose one of the generalizations from *Rescuing Stranded Whales* listed below. Write the generalization in the top rectangle of the graphic organizer. Then find at least three facts in the story that support the generalization. Write those facts in the boxes below the generalization.

Possible Generalizations

A stranded whale is in great danger unless it is rescued.

There are many things to do to help a stranded whale.

There are many steps in bringing a stranded whale to an aquarium.

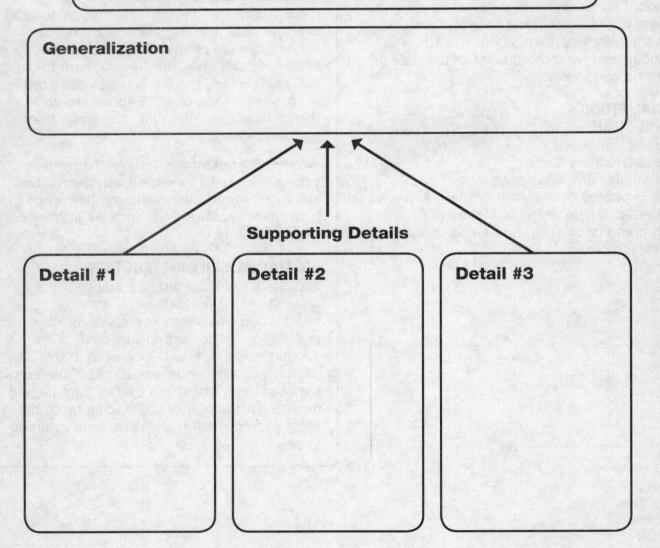

Generalization

Supporting Details

Detail #1

Detail #2

Detail #3

© Pearson Education 3

Name _____

Vocabulary

Directions Read the groups of words in each box. Write the vocabulary word that fits with each group.

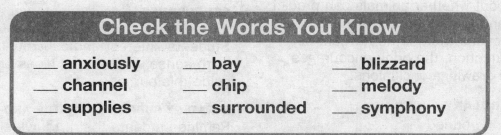

Check the Words You Know

___ anxiously   ___ bay   ___ blizzard
___ channel   ___ chip   ___ melody
___ supplies   ___ surrounded   ___ symphony

1. broken   bits   pieces

_____

2. partly enclosed body of water
cove   inlet

_____

3. tune   song   music

_____

4. deep water   basin   body of water

_____

5. encircled   enclosed   enveloped

_____

6. nervously   fearfully   with panic

_____

7. snowstorm   storm
heavy snowfall

_____

8. collection   necessary things
reserve

_____

9. musical composition   concert
classical music

_____

Do Animals Have a Sixth Sense?

SUMMARY This book gives students fascinating information about whether animals can predict earthquakes and volcanos, and why this could be helpful. Because there is no firm answer to the title's question, the book encourages reasoning and drawing conclusions.

LESSON VOCABULARY

beneath	buried
chimney	earthquakes
fireworks	force
surface	tremble
volcano	

INTRODUCE THE BOOK

INTRODUCE THE TITLE AND AUTHOR Discuss with students the title and the author of *Do Animals Have a Sixth Sense?* Ask students why they think the author titled the reader with a question and whether that indicates that students might find answers to it as they read. Direct students' attention to the "Science" triangle on the cover and ask them how they imagine something like a "sixth sense" might be scientific.

BUILD BACKGROUND Discuss with students if they have ever seen or heard of animals behaving strangely and what they imagine that might mean. Ask students what they know about the "sixth sense," and discuss the possibility of such a thing.

PREVIEW/USE TEXT FEATURES Invite students to look at the photograph and captions through-out the reader. Ask students what information these elements provide and how they help students prepare themselves for what might come next in the selection.

READ THE BOOK

SET PURPOSE Have students set a purpose for reading *Do Animals Have a Sixth Sense?* Students' interest and curiosity in animals, a sixth sense, and natural disasters should help guide this purpose.

STRATEGY SUPPORT: MONITOR AND FIX UP Remind students that if they feel their comprehension is breaking down as they read, they can monitor and use fix-up strategies like reading ahead to find the answer, or rereading and reviewing to make sure they didn't miss any information. Students can also adjust their reading rate or seek help from other people. Remind students that these skills can help them find answers to questions or problems they might have in their reading. Encourage students to take notes as they read to help them to organize their thoughts and track their comprehension.

COMPREHENSION QUESTIONS

PAGE 5 How do certain animals act before natural disasters? *(Dogs howl, birds have trouble perching, cats hide, and bees leave their hives.)*

PAGE 8 Why is it difficult to know what animals sense? *(They can't talk to us.)*

PAGE 9 Read the caption above the photo. Answer the question by referring to the text. *(The dog might sense an earthquake coming.)*

REVISIT THE BOOK

READER RESPONSE

1. Both can be dangerous and destroy people and animals. Earthquakes happen when there is a sudden movement of the Earth's crust. Volcanoes happen when magma builds up and mixes with gas from the volcano.
2. Possible response: Did the Alaska earthquake happen before I was born? Yes. I found on page 8 that it happened in 1983.
3. Possible responses: shake, move, shudder, quake
4. Mongolia and India are shown. Mongolia is north of China, and India is southwest of China.

EXTEND UNDERSTANDING Encourage students to look at the captions under the photographs, many of which are in the form of questions. Ask: How do these questions help you think about what you are reading and what you may want to find out next?

RESPONSE OPTIONS

WRITING Suggest that students imagine they are a cat or a dog and are sensing that an earthquake is about to happen. Ask students to write a story from the animal's point of view, describing what he or she might do to get a human's attention. Encourage students to read their stories to the class.

SCIENCE CONNECTION

TIME FOR **Science**

To gain more insight into what an animal might be feeling or thinking, suggest students read a story that is told from the viewpoint of an animal and then write a short report about the book.

Skill Work

TEACH/REVIEW VOCABULARY
Review vocabulary words with students. Then play a game of hangman on the board, using the definitions as clues to the words.

ELL Review vocabulary words with students. To connect students to the vocabulary words, ask: If your dog *buried* a bone, where would the bone be? Do this with the other words.

TARGET SKILL AND STRATEGY

COMPARE AND CONTRAST Remind students that *comparing and contrasting* are ways of determining how things are alike and how they are different. Create a graphic organizer, and ask students to compare and contrast third grade to second grade. Then suggest that as they read, students make a graphic organizer to compare and contrast the ways various animals react prior to natural disasters.

MONITOR AND FIX UP Remind students that *monitoring* is being aware of when their understanding of the text breaks down. When students feel that they do not understand a passage, they should ask themselves: *What is the author trying to tell me, what does this mean, and do I understand?* Suggest that as students read, they summarize facts and details to organize their ideas. Then they should fix up their understanding of the story.

ADDITIONAL SKILL INSTRUCTION

DRAW CONCLUSIONS Remind students that to *draw a conclusion* is to think about facts and details and decide something about them. Give students a series of facts and details about various animals and encourage them to draw conclusions. Suggest that as they read, students write down facts and details in a graphic organizer and draw conclusions based on their reading.

Name _____

Compare and Contrast

- When you **compare** two or more things, you think about how they are alike and how they are different.
- When you **contrast** two or more things, you only think about how they are different.

Directions Reread the story *Do Animals Have a Sixth Sense?* Then use the chart below to fill in the facts about the behaviors of dogs, cats, and bees before a natural disaster.

Dogs	Cats	Bees
1. _____ 2. _____	3. _____	4. _____

5. Write a general statement about how animals behave in similar ways before a natural disaster.

   _____

   _____

   _____

6. Write a general statement about the different behaviors of animals before a natural disaster.

   _____

   _____

   _____

Name _____

Vocabulary

Directions Draw a line from the first part of a word to its second part to form a whole word.

Check the Words You Know

___beneath	___buried	___chimney
___earthquakes	___fireworks	___force
___surface	___tremble	___volcano

1. be   **a.** ied

2. chim   **b.** quakes

3. fire   **c.** ble

4. sur   **d.** cano

5. for   **e.** ce

6. bur   **f.** neath

7. earth   **g.** ney

8. trem   **h.** works

9. vol   **i.** face

Directions Two of the words above are compound words. Write their parts and the compound words they form below.

10. _____ + _____ = _____

11. _____ + _____ = _____

The Lesson of Icarus

SUMMARY *The Lesson of Icarus* retells the ancient Greek myth about the boy who flew too high. In the myth, Daedalus and his son Icarus have been imprisoned by King Minos. In order to escape, Daedalus and Icarus make wings of wax and fly from the prison tower. Icarus enjoys flying so much, he forgets his father's warning and flies too close to the sun. The boy's wings melt, and he falls into the sea and drowns.

LESSON VOCABULARY

attention	complained
drifting	giggle
glaring	looping
struggled	swooping

INTRODUCE THE BOOK

INTRODUCE THE TITLE AND AUTHOR Discuss with students the title and the author of *The Lesson of Icarus*. Provide students with the correct pronunciation of "Icarus" (IK-ah-rus), and explain that the word is the name of a character. Point out the genre, and explain to students that a myth is a type of story that people told long ago to teach lessons or answer questions about things that people could not explain. Have volunteers briefly describe myths they have read or heard.

BUILD BACKGROUND Invite students to talk about times when they did not listen to an adult's advice or warnings about something. Ask: Was there ever a time when an adult gave you advice or warned you about something? Why do you think the adult gave you this advice or warning? Did you listen to the advice or warning? Why or why not? What happened when you did or did not listen?

PREVIEW Look through the pictures on the cover and inside the book with students. Talk about the characters in the pictures. Ask:

What do you notice about the characters' clothing? *(Possible responses: They are wearing some sort of cloth and sandals.)* What do the clothes tell you about the characters and the story? *(Possible responses: The characters might be from Rome; the story takes place a long time ago.)* Explain to students that this story is a myth from Ancient Greece and is more than 2,000 years old. Discuss with students anything else they notice about the pictures.

READ THE BOOK

SET PURPOSE Have students set a purpose for reading by completing the following sentence: I want to read this myth because I want to find out _____.

STRATEGY SUPPORT: ANSWER QUESTIONS To help students answer the cause-and-effect questions about Icarus, have students write down the page number where the author tells what happened to Icarus. Also have students write down the page number where the author describes why this happened.

COMPREHENSION QUESTIONS

PAGE 5 Why did Daedalus tell Theseus to tie a long string onto the prison door? *(so he could follow the trail of string out of the maze)*

PAGES 6–7 What happens to Daedalus and Icarus? Why does this happen? *(King Minos puts them in prison because he thinks Daedalus helped Theseus run away with the princess.)*

PAGE 9 Why does Daedalus warn his son not to fly too close to the sun? *(The sun will melt the wax wings, and Icarus will crash.)*

PAGE 11 What happens at the end of the plot of the story? *(The wings melt, and Icarus falls into the sea and drowns.)*

REVISIT THE BOOK

READER RESPONSE

1. What Happened: The wings fell apart. Why It Happened: The Sun melted the wax that held the feathers together.
2. Theseus came to slay the Minotaur and marry the princess; page 4.
3. Possible response: swooping, looping, drifting; soaring, gliding, flapping
4. Possible response: Yes, because the warning would have frightened me.

EXTEND UNDERSTANDING Remind students that Ancient Greeks often told myths to teach a lesson. Have students reread *What Myths Tell Us* on page 12 of the book and answer the questions at the end of the section. *(Possible responses: The value of listening to adults; it was first told to remind young people to listen to adults or possibly suffer consequences.)*

RESPONSE OPTIONS

WRITING Have students think about the myth they just read and consider the situations they discussed in the *Build Background* section of the lesson. Tell students to write a paragraph about a time when an adult gave them advice or a warning. Have students explain in their paragraphs whether they listened to the advice and what happened because they did or did not do what the adult suggested.

SOCIAL STUDIES CONNECTION

Have students read other ancient myths. Tell each student to write a *story map* of the myth in which they list the characters, the important events in the plot, and what the myth teaches.

Time For SOCIAL STUDIES

Skill Work

TEACH/REVIEW VOCABULARY

Before defining the vocabulary words, assign words to groups of students. Have groups make educated guesses about the pronunciations and meanings of their words. Suggest that students break the words into their parts, or syllables, and think about how the parts or the whole words look or sound like other words they know. After each group has analyzed its word, have groups share their guesses with the class. Then provide correct definitions and pronunciations.

ELL Point out to students some common pronunciation rules that apply to the vocabulary words (for example, the sound of double "o" and the short vowel pronunciation before a double consonant, like in *giggle*).

TARGET SKILL AND STRATEGY

CAUSE AND EFFECT Explain to students that usually there is a reason *(cause)* why something happens *(effect)* in a story. Point out that often what happens *follows* why the event happened. Direct students to look for what happens to Icarus and why.

ANSWER QUESTIONS Remind students that when they *answer questions* about a story, they may find the answers in one sentence in a story, or they may have to search in several different places. Suggest that knowing where to look for answers to questions can help them figure out what happened to a character and why.

ADDITIONAL SKILL INSTRUCTION

PLOT Explain to students that *plot* is the pattern of events in a story, and that stories almost always have a beginning, middle, and end. On the board, place five important story events on moveable sentence cards. Put the cards out of the order of events in the story. Tell students to look for these important story events as they read. When students have finished reading the selection, have volunteers put the events in the correct order in which they happen.

Cause and Effect

- A **cause** is why something happened. An **effect** is what happened. Look for clue words.

Directions Use the story *The Lesson of Icarus* to complete the chart below. For each event that happened in the story, fill in why the event happened.

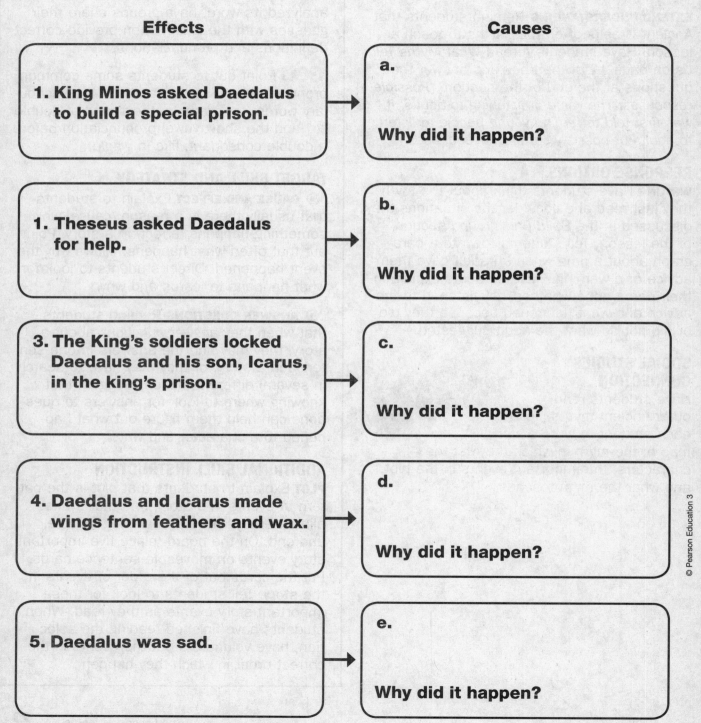

Effects

Causes

1. King Minos asked Daedalus to build a special prison.

a.

Why did it happen?

1. Theseus asked Daedalus for help.

b.

Why did it happen?

3. The King's soldiers locked Daedalus and his son, Icarus, in the king's prison.

c.

Why did it happen?

4. Daedalus and Icarus made wings from feathers and wax.

d.

Why did it happen?

5. Daedalus was sad.

e.

Why did it happen?

© Pearson Education 3

Name _____

Vocabulary

Directions Choose the word from the box that best completes each sentence. Write the word on the line.

Check the Words You Know

___attention
___complained
___drifting
___giggle
___glaring
___looping
___struggled
___swooping

1. The boat was _____ out to sea.

2. No one _____ when school closed early because of the snowstorm.

3. I always let out a _____ when my brother does silly tricks.

4. The bird was _____ high and low searching for insects to eat.

5. I had to close my eyes when I walked out into the _____ sunshine.

6. People need to pay _____ and look both ways when crossing the street.

7. The monkey hung from the tree by _____ its tail around a branch.

8. Children _____ to put on their coats and hats before going out to play.

Measuring the Weather

SUMMARY This nonfiction reader describes aspects of weather—temperature, wind, precipitation, and air pressure—and the tools meteorologists use to measure these phenomena.

LESSON VOCABULARY

average	depth
desert	outrun
peak	tides
waterfalls	

INTRODUCE THE BOOK

INTRODUCE THE TITLE AND AUTHOR Discuss with students the title and the author of *Measuring the Weather.* Point out the genre and content triangle and discuss with students what sort of information might be included in the book. Ask: What tools do we use for measuring? *(Possible responses: rulers, scales, measuring cups and spoons, thermometers)*

BUILD BACKGROUND Put the word *weather* at the center of a concept web on the board. Invite students to brainstorm the words and ideas that come to mind when they think of the word *weather.* Review the measuring tools students suggested when talking about the title of the selection. Ask students what measuring tools they think are used to measure weather.

PREVIEW/USE TEXT FEATURES Tell students to skim through the text by looking at the pictures. Have students focus on the pictures of instruments and point out any that they recognize. Explain that all of the instruments shown are used to measure weather. Then have students predict what some of the unfamiliar instruments measure, based on what is shown in the nearby photographs.

READ THE BOOK

SET PURPOSE Have students set a purpose for reading the selection by completing the following sentence: I want to read this book because I want to find out more about _____. Tell students to fill in the blank with a topic about measuring the weather.

STRATEGY SUPPORT: ASK QUESTIONS Provide students with guidelines for asking questions about comparisons and contrasts they find or make about topics in the text. For example, students may fill in the blank in either of the following questions: How are _____ and _____ alike? How are _____ and _____ different? *(Possible responses: thermometers and barometers; Fahrenheit and Celsius)*

COMPREHENSION QUESTIONS

PAGE 5 Contrast Celsius and Fahrenheit thermometers. *(The freezing point on a Celsius thermometer is 0 degrees, but on a Fahrenheit thermometer it is 32 degrees.)*

PAGE 7 What question could you ask about wind that is answered on this page? *(Possible response: What is a wind named after?)*

PAGE 9 What does an anemometer use to measure the speed of wind? *(cups that spin)*

PAGE 11 What is the main idea of this page? *(Possible response: You can make your own rain gauge to measure how much rain has fallen in inches.)*

PAGE 12 What comparison does the author make on this page? *(Thermometers, weather vanes, anemometers, rain gauges, and barometers all measure weather.)*

REVISIT THE BOOK

READER RESPONSE

1. *Anemometer:* measures wind speed, has cups; *Weather Vane:* measures wind direction, has arrow; *Both:* measure wind
2. Possible response: How fast do winds blow in a hurricane?
3. *Waterfalls, yardsticks;* Sentences will vary.
4. The wind is coming from the south. The arrow is pointing to "S."

EXTEND UNDERSTANDING Explain that authors often include photographs in nonfiction books to help readers understand what happens in the text. Discuss with students how the pictures of the weather instruments in this selection helped them better understand the tools and how they work.

RESPONSE OPTIONS

WORD WORK Provide students with the etymology of the word *meteorology*: *meteor-* meaning "things in the air" and *–ology* meaning "the science of." Have students look up the definition of *meteorology* in a dictionary and write a brief paragraph comparing today's definition of the word with its origin.

SCIENCE CONNECTION

Have students create their own weather stations at home that include a thermometer and rain gauge (a simple can or jug to collect water). Tell students to take readings of the thermometer and rain gauges once a day every day for a week and chart their readings in a table. Have students compare tables at the end of the week and plot their readings on classroom graphs.

Skill Work

TEACH/REVIEW VOCABULARY

List the vocabulary words on the board and go over the definitions. Divide the class into groups, and assign each group a vocabulary word. Have each group create clues for its word. Clues may relate to the meaning, spelling, part of speech, or pronunciation of the word. Then have groups give their clues to the class while other students try to guess the word.

ELL Have ELL students work in pairs to illustrate the vocabulary words. Assign the more difficult words, such as *average* and *depth,* to more advanced English-language speakers.

TARGET SKILL AND STRATEGY

COMPARE AND CONTRAST Remind students that to *compare* two or more things, they describe how those things are alike. To *contrast* those things means to describe only how they are different. As they read, have students look for one example of a comparison or a contrast in the text.

ASK QUESTIONS Point out to students that when they *ask questions* about a text, they are helping themselves better understand and remember what they read. Remind students that they can ask questions to compare and contrast things in a story. Have students pose a question that may be used to identify the comparison or contrast they find in the text.

ADDITIONAL SKILL INSTRUCTION

MAIN IDEA AND DETAILS Review with students that a *main idea* is the most important idea about a topic. *Supporting details* tell more about the main idea. On the board, list the weather instruments from the selection. Have students choose one instrument to focus on. As students read, have them look for the main idea about their topic. When students have finished reading, tell them to write the main idea in a sentence. Then have them find two supporting details in the book that tell more about this main idea.

Compare and Contrast

- A **comparison** shows how two or more things are alike. A **contrast** shows how two or more things are different.
- Clue words such as **like** and **as** show comparisons. Clue words such as **but** and **unlike** show contrasts.

Directions Complete the chart below using information from *Measuring the Weather*. The first row has been done for you.

Instrument	What It Measures	Unit of Measurement
Thermometer	temperature	degrees Celsius or Fahrenheit
Anemometer	1.	2.
Rain Gauge	3.	4.

Directions Complete the sentences that compare and contrast. Write your answers on the lines provided.

5. A thermometer and a barometer are alike because

_____

A thermometer and a barometer are different because

_____

_____

Name _____

Vocabulary

Directions Draw lines to match the words with their definitions.

1. depth   **a.** the pointed top of a mountain or hill

2. outrun   **b.** the distance from the top to the bottom

3. average   **c.** dry, sandy region without water or trees

4. peak   **d.** to run faster than someone or something

5. desert   **e.** the quantity found by dividing the sum of all the quantities by the number of quantities

6. waterfalls   **f.** the rise and fall of the ocean

7. tides   **g.** a stream of water that falls from a high place

Directions Imagine you are an explorer. Write a brief paragraph about one of your adventures using the words *desert, outrun, peak, tides,* and *waterfalls.*

_____

_____

_____

_____

_____

_____

The Rock Kit

SUMMARY In *The Rock Kit*, a mother teaches her two children everything her father taught her about rocks. The selection describes the three kinds of rocks that make up the Earth's crust and gives examples of each.

LESSON VOCABULARY

attic	board	chores
customers	label	spare
stamps		

INTRODUCE THE BOOK

INTRODUCE THE TITLE AND AUTHOR Discuss with students the title and the author of *The Rock Kit*. Ask: What does the word *kit* make you think of? (Possible response: a box with materials to make something) What do you think might be inside a rock kit? (Possible response: rocks and other things to help you make something with the rocks) Explain to students that in this story, a *kit* is a collection.

ELL For students unfamiliar with the word *kit*, point out that many words have more than one meaning. Introduce students to the multiple meanings of the word *kit*, and reinforce the Build Background activity by emphasizing the meaning used in this story.

BUILD BACKGROUND Bring in a variety of rocks to share with the class. If possible, include some examples of rocks mentioned in the reader. Pass the rocks around the class and have students describe what they see and feel. Invite volunteers to share what they know about the different types of rocks found on Earth. Write their ideas on the board. Point out that students will read about Earth's variety of rocks in this story.

PREVIEW/USE TEXT FEATURES Have students look through the pictures in the book. Discuss with students what the people in the pictures seem to be doing. Then focus on the rock diagrams and pictures.

READ THE BOOK

SET PURPOSE To guide students in setting their purposes for reading, have them look at the W section of the class KWL chart about rocks. Tell each student to choose one fact they want to know about rocks and use it to complete the following sentence: I want to read this story because I want to know _____.

STRATEGY SUPPORT: PRIOR KNOWLEDGE To help students activate prior knowledge, set up a classroom KWL (Know, Want to Know, Learned) chart on the chalkboard. Use students' ideas about rocks from the Build Background section as the Know part of the chart. Have students suggest facts they want to know about rocks. When students have finished reading, have them fill in the Learned part of the chart with facts about rocks from the text.

COMPREHENSION QUESTIONS

PAGE 3 Can you find a statement of opinion on this page? Who says it? (*Mom says cleaning out the attic will be fun.*)

PAGES 6–7 Is there anything on this page that you already know something about? How does your knowledge help you understand the information here? (*Possible response: I know that when volcanoes erupt, lava comes out. Since I already know what lava is, I understand better how lava becomes igneous rock.*)

PAGE 9 What is one type of sedimentary rock? How does its name tell you something about its qualities? (*sandstone; it's soft like sand*)

PAGE 11 What generalization can you find on this page? (*Possible response: Marble is usually whiter.*)

REVISIT THE BOOK

READER RESPONSE

1. Possible response: All three rocks are found in Earth's crust.
2. Possible response: I knew that limestone was a type of sedimentary rock. I read about it in a library book.
3. Possible response: The attic in our house is always cold because there is no heat up there.
4. the core

EXTEND UNDERSTANDING

Review with students the KWL chart on the board. Look through all the facts about rocks that students wanted to know. Then fill in what they learned about rocks. Have students tell where they found their facts in the book. Discuss where students might look to find out more about rocks.

RESPONSE OPTIONS

WRITING Have students research different types of rocks. Tell students to create an encyclopedia entry for their rock in which they describe the rock's qualities; tell whether the rock is igneous, sedimentary, or metamorphic; and explain where the rock is usually found. Collect the entries into a classroom rock encyclopedia.

SCIENCE CONNECTIONS

Have students make categories for the various types of rocks in their rock encyclopedia. Tell students to start by grouping their rocks as either igneous or sedimentary or metamorphic. Then have students come up with other categories for the rocks based on their characteristics or where they are found. Use the category lists as an index for the rock encyclopedia.

Skill Work

TEACH/REVIEW VOCABULARY

Divide students into groups and assign one vocabulary word to each group. Have members of the group find the word's definition in the dictionary; write a sentence for the word; illustrate the word; and share the definition, sentence, and illustration with the class.

TARGET SKILL AND STRATEGY

GENERALIZE Remind students that sometimes they can *generalize,* or make a statement about several ideas or things in a book. The statement can tell how the ideas or things are all alike or mostly alike, for example, "All animals that have feathers are birds." Or, the statement can tell about how some ideas or things in a text are all or mostly different, for example, "No animals without feathers are birds." As students read, have them think about a statement that they can make about how the rocks in the book are all or mostly alike or different.

PRIOR KNOWLEDGE Point out to students that thinking about what they already know about a topic can help them understand what they read. Explain that activating *prior knowledge* can help them see how ideas or things in the story are alike or different. Remind students of the list compiled of what they already know about rocks gathered during the Build Background. As students read, have them take note of how they used this information to help them understand the text.

ADDITIONAL SKILL INSTRUCTION

FACT AND OPINION Remind students that a statement of *fact* can be proved true or false, but a statement of *opinion* is a person's ideas or feelings about a topic. Remind students that they do not actually have to prove a statement of fact true or false, but just be able to decide whether it can be checked. Have students look for statements of fact and of opinion in the text as they read.

Generalize

- A **generalization** is a broad statement or rule that applies to many examples.
- A **valid generalization** is adequately supported by specific facts and by logic.

Directions Read the passage below.

"Granite is igneous rock. Granite is usually gray. It can have tiny white and black crystals. Some granite has pink crystals," Mom said as she held up a rock for Tina to see.

"Another type of rock is sedimentary rock. Sandstone is sedimentary rock. Rivers carry sand to lakes and seas. Layers of sand settle to the bottom. The top layers of sand press down on the bottom layers. This pressing turns sand into sandstone. Sandstone is soft and sandy," Mom explained.

"Limestone is a sedimentary rock too. It is made from sea animals' skeletons. Sometimes you can see the skeletons in the rock. Limestone is often white. It can be pink, tan, or other colors too."

Directions Make a generalization about each of the rocks in this passage.

Granite	
Sandstone	
Limestone	

Name _____

Vocabulary

Directions Unscramble each of the following words.

Check the Words You Know

___attic	___board	___chores	___customer
___label	___spare	___stamps	

1. rhesoc   _____

2. llbae   _____

3. itcat   _____

4. pastsm   _____

5. odrab   _____

4. reaps   _____

5. stromcuse   _____

Directions Use four of the words that you unscrambled in a paragraph about something you did on a Saturday afternoon. Your paragraph can tell about something real or imaginary.

_____

_____

_____

_____

The English Channel

SUMMARY This nonfiction reader tells about some of the earliest attempts to swim across the English Channel and highlights a few of the cross-channel record holders. The book also describes the conditions in the Channel that make it such a challenging body of water for swimmers.

LESSON VOCABULARY

celebrate	continued
current	drowned
medal	stirred
strokes	

INTRODUCE THE BOOK

INTRODUCE THE TITLE AND AUTHOR Discuss the title and the author of *The English Channel*. Ask students to predict what the English Channel is, based on the cover photographs. Discuss with students who the woman pictured on the cover might be.

BUILD BACKGROUND By a show of hands, find out how many students in the class like to swim. Have volunteers talk about where they like to swim, such as in pools, lakes, or the ocean. Tell students to describe what they like most about swimming in these places and what they like the least.

ELL Have ELL students describe their favorite swimming places in their home countries and compare them with places where they have gone swimming in the United States.

PREVIEW/USE TEXT FEATURES Explain to students that the selection is about a body of water called the English Channel. Have students look at the maps on pages 3 and 6. Discuss with students what conditions in the Channel might be like. Then have students skim through the rest of the pictures in the book. Ask students to describe the people in the pictures and what they seem to be doing.

READ THE BOOK

SET PURPOSE Invite students to look at the cover of the reader once again. Help them to set a purpose for reading by having them complete the following statement: "I would like to read this book about the English Channel to find out more about _____."

STRATEGY SUPPORT: MONITOR AND FIX UP As they read, have students write down one place where they monitor their reading and find that they do not understand something in the text. Tell students to write down the fix-up strategy that they use to help their comprehension, such as rereading, reading on, or slowing down. Have volunteers describe the fix-up strategies they use.

COMPREHENSION QUESTIONS

PAGES 4–5 What general statement can you make about the English Channel? *(Possible response: The English Channel is always difficult to swim.)*

PAGES 8–9 Is there anything you find confusing on these pages? What fix-up strategy can you use? *(Possible response: I was confused about how Gertrude Ederle broke the men's record by only two hours when Matthew Webb swam the Channel in 22 hours. Then I reread and realized that Ederle broke the men's record of her period, not Webb's old record.)*

PAGE 10 Find a statement of fact on this page. How do you know it is a statement of fact? *(Possible response: Others are part of a team of two or more swimmers. It can be proved true or false by checking in a book.)*

PAGE 12 Find a statement of opinion in the first paragraph on this page and tell how you know it is an opinion. *(Possible response: That difficult task seems like something to celebrate. It's an opinion because it's the author's belief about why someone should celebrate.)*

REVISIT THE BOOK

READER RESPONSE

1. Possible responses: Facts: The English Channel is a narrow body of water (p. 3). Many kinds of goods are carried through the Channel each day (p. 4). Opinions: Some swimmers see these wild waters as a challenge (p. 7). That was an awesome feat (p. 9)!
2. The Channel is more than 21 miles across (p. 4). The waters are rough and choppy (p. 6). The currents are very strong (p. 7).
3. *Stir* may also mean "to mix." Possible responses: The wind stirred the leaves gently. She stirred the cake batter until it was smooth.
4. Student responses will vary.

EXTEND UNDERSTANDING Explain to students that *graphic sources* are visual aids, such as maps, graphs, time lines, and pictures with captions, that help the reader understand the text. Point out that sometimes graphics provide additional information. Have students look through the pictures and captions in *The English Channel* and find one piece of information that they learned from the captions that was not in the text. Invite volunteers to share their answers.

RESPONSE OPTIONS

WRITING Tell students to think of an amazing feat that they might try, such as swimming underwater the entire length of a pool. Have students write a plan to prepare for their feat, including information on training, diet, and equipment.

SOCIAL STUDIES CONNECTION

Time For SOCIAL STUDIES

Explain to students that a *strait* is a type of channel. Have students research other famous channels and straits from around the globe, including the Bering Strait, the Bosporus Strait, and the Strait of Magellan. Tell students to write brief reports describing the geography and conditions of their channels, as well as how people use them today.

Skill Work

TEACH/REVIEW VOCABULARY

Write a sentence for each word on the chalkboard. Have volunteers guess the meanings of the words by using context clues. Then have other students look up each word in the dictionary and tell the class the definition.

TARGET SKILL AND STRATEGY

FACT AND OPINION Explain to students that a *statement of fact* is a statement that can be proved true or false. A *statement of opinion* is a person's beliefs or ideas about something. Point out that as readers they just need to know that the statement can be checked by looking in reference sources, by asking an expert, or by observing. Give examples of statements of facts and opinions, and discuss with students how to distinguish each. Then tell students to look for at least one statement of fact and one statement of opinion in the reader.

MONITOR AND FIX UP Review with students that they should *monitor* their reading, or check their understanding of the text. Tell students that to monitor understanding, they should ask questions such as "Do I understand this?" Remind students that they can use a strategy to *"fix up"* their reading, such as rereading, reading on, or reading slower. Explain that using monitor and fix-up strategies may help them find facts and opinions in the text. Tell students to use a monitor and fix-up strategy whenever they are unsure about something they read.

ADDITIONAL SKILL INSTRUCTION

GENERALIZE Explain to students that sometimes authors make a statement about several ideas or things in a book. The statement can tell how the ideas or things are all alike or mostly alike or how they are all or mostly different. Provide examples of generalizations that state how things in a group are alike or different. As students read, have them look for a general statement that the author makes about the English Channel.

Name _____

Fact and Opinion

- A statement of fact is a statement that can be proved true or false. You can check a statement of fact by looking in reference sources, asking an expert, or observing.
- A statement of opinion is a person's beliefs or ideas about something. You cannot prove whether it is true or false.

Directions Decide whether each sentence below is a statement of fact or opinion. Write your answer on the line.

1. The English Channel is about 350 miles long.

_____

2. The English Channel is quite shallow.

_____

3. There is always a chance that a swimmer could drown.

_____

4. In 1926, Gertrude Ederle of the United States became the first woman to swim across the English Channel.

_____

5. But if you have the stamina, the skill, and the desire for a challenge, you might consider swimming as an alternate way to cross the English Channel.

_____

© Pearson Education 3

Name _____

Vocabulary

Directions Fill in each column of the chart below with the correct words from the box You may use a word more than once.

┌─────────────────────────────────────┐
│ **Check the Words You Know**   │
│   │
│ ___celebrate   ___continued   │
│ ___current   ___drowned   │
│ ___medal   ___stirred   │
│ ___strokes   │
└─────────────────────────────────────┘

Singular Nouns	Verbs in Past Tense	Words with Endings
1.	3.	6.
2.	4.	7.
	5.	8.
		9.

Directions Write an original paragraph about something special that you did. How did you celebrate? Describe your accomplishment and use the word *celebrate* in your paragraph.

_____

_____

_____

_____

_____

_____

Buck's Way

SUMMARY This fictional story is a funny retelling of *The Ugly Ducking*. It gives students information about being proud of who they are and puts forth the idea that things that seem to be holding you back can often be a benefit.

LESSON VOCABULARY

clutched	echoed
gully	reeds
scrambled	valley

INTRODUCE THE BOOK

INTRODUCE THE TITLE AND AUTHOR Discuss the title and author of the book *Buck's Way* with students. Ask students what the title makes them think the story might be about. Direct students' attention to the cover illustration and discuss what is happening in the picture and how it might relate to the story.

BUILD BACKGROUND Ask students if they have ever been teased for doing something differently than everybody else. Discuss how students handled the teasing, and then suggest why doing things differently can actually be beneficial.

PREVIEW Invite students to look through the illustrations of the story. Ask students if they can get an idea about the story just from looking at the pictures, then ask students how the drawings help them determine if this will be a funny or sad story.

READ THE BOOK

SET PURPOSE Have students set a purpose for reading Buck's Way. Students' interest in how to handle teasing and their love of animal stories should help guide this purpose.

STRATEGY SUPPORT: GRAPHIC ORGANIZERS Suggest that as students read *Buck's Way*, they create two or three graphic organizers to enhance their understanding of the story. For example, they could use a story map for the plot; a time line for the sequence of events; character webs to describe Buck, Quack, and the coach; or a problem-and-solution or cause-and-effect chart to understand the action in the story.

COMPREHENSION QUESTIONS

PAGE 3 What was the big problem Buck had to solve in this story? *(He was being teased because of the way he was swimming.)*

PAGE 7 How else do you think Buck could have handled the teasing? *(Possible responses: He did the right thing. He could have kept swimming and ignored them.)*

PAGE 9 What does the coach's opinion tell you about how you see yourself and how others see you? *(Possible response: You should be proud of being different even though others may make fun of you.)*

PAGES 10–11 Using a graphic organizer, list the steps of how Buck and Quack became friends. *(Step 1: Buck joined the team and won every race. Step 2: Buck became famous for his swimming style. Step 3: Quack got Buck's autograph and asked if he could learn Buck's special style. Step 4: Buck said he would teach him.)*

REVISIT THE BOOK

READER RESPONSE

1. Buck meets the swim team coach. The meeting gives him a solution to his problem.
2. Problem: Buck was teased because of his unusual swimming style. Solution: Excelling on the swim team gained him respect, and the teasing stopped.
3. Sentences should reflect understanding of word meaning and of past tense.
4. By forgiving Quack, Buck taught him that kindness is important. Possible response: I would have forgiven Quack.

EXTEND UNDERSTANDING Remind students that the sequence of events is the order in which things happen in a story. Ask students to make a time line of all the events that happen to Buck, and then discuss how one event leads to another and then finally to the happy ending.

RESPONSE OPTIONS

WRITING Suggest students imagine they are Quack, and have them write an apology to Buck.

LITERATURE CONNECTION

Have students reread *The Ugly Duckling* and then ask them to compare the story with *Buck's Way*.

Skill Work

TEACH/REVIEW VOCABULARY

Hide definitions for the vocabulary words around the classroom near, on, or under things that start with the same letter as the vocabulary word—for example the definition for *scrambled* could be hidden by the sharpener. Tell students each word, and then have them look at its definition.

ELL Have students write the definition of each vocabulary word on one side of a card and the word on the other. They can use the cards to test themselves or other English Language Learners.

TARGET SKILL AND STRATEGY

PLOT AND THEME Remind students that the *plot* is the important parts of a story. These parts include the beginning, middle, and end. Review a story students have recently read and discuss the beginning, middle, and end of the story. Then ask students to identify the big idea of the story. Suggest that as they read *Buck's Way* students take notes that name the important events in the story.

GRAPHIC ORGANIZERS Remind students that *graphic organizers* are diagrams and charts that help readers understand what they read. Suggest that as students read *Buck's Way*, they make a story map to write down the important events that happen at the beginning, middle, and end of the story. Remind students that graphic organizers can help them determine the story's plot as well as its big idea.

ADDITIONAL SKILL INSTRUCTION

CHARACTERIZATION Remind students that a character is the person or animal who does the action or talking in the book. Invite students to draw a character map of Buck, with the headings "What Buck Thinks of Himself," "What Others Think or Say About Buck," and "What Buck Does." Suggest that as students read the book, they fill in information from the story under each heading.

Name _____

Plot and Theme

- A story's **plot** is the important parts of a story. These parts include the beginning, middle, and end.
- A story's **theme** is the **big idea** of a story. It can be stated in one sentence. It is an idea that the author would like you to learn.

Directions Write the answers to these questions on the lines below.

1. How would the story of *Buck's Way* be different if Buck had not joined the swim team?

_____

_____

2. What else could Buck have done to solve his problem?

_____

_____

3. How do you think the story might have ended?

_____

_____

Directions What is the message of *Buck's Way?* What does the author want you to learn by thinking about the story? Retell the story of *Buck's Way* in your own words. Your last sentence should be the message of the story.

4–5. _____

_____

_____

_____

_____

_____

Name _____

Vocabulary

Directions Write the definition of each word in the
space provided.

1. clutched

_____

2. echoed

_____

3. gully

_____

4. reeds

_____

5. scrambled

_____

6. valley

_____

Directions Write a short story about Buck using four words from the word box.

7–10. _____

_____

_____

_____

_____

East Meets West: Japan and America

SUMMARY This selection gives students a look at the differences and similarities between Japanese and American culture.

LESSON VOCABULARY

cotton	festival
graceful	handkerchief
pace	pale
rhythm	snug

INTRODUCE THE BOOK

INTRODUCE THE TITLE AND AUTHOR Discuss with students the title and the author of the selection *East Meets West: Japan and America*. Direct students' attention to the term *social studies* in the triangle on the cover and ask them how they imagine this topic will fit into social studies. Ask students if they know what the objects on the cover are.

BUILD BACKGROUND Discuss with students what they know about Japan and Japanese culture. Ask students if they have ever eaten Japanese food or flown Japanese kites or heard Japanese words such as *yen* and *sushi*.

PREVIEW/ILLUSTRATIONS Invite students to look at the illustrations in the selection. Ask students if anything in the photographs is familiar to them, and if not, what in each photograph looks interesting to them.

READ THE BOOK

SET PURPOSE Have students set a purpose for reading *East Meets West: Japan and America*. Students' curiosity about Japan and other foreign cultures should guide this purpose.

STRATEGY SUPPORT: PREDICT/CONFIRM PREDICTIONS As students read, remind them to use their graphic organizers to make predictions and to check back to see if their predictions were correct or not. If needed, suggest students revise their predictions based on any new information they might read.

COMPREHENSION QUESTIONS

PAGES 5 AND 7 What can you generalize about the fact that Japanese have holidays for both their sons and daughters? *(They love their children and want them to be happy and strong.)*

PAGE 10 Compare and contrast Japanese and American comics. *(Both Americans and Japanese enjoy comics. Japanese comics are read from right to left, and they have their own style.)*

PAGE 12 Predict how you would enjoy learning a new game in Japan. *(Possible responses: I would love it, I would have fun, I would be confused.)*

PAGE 12 What do you like about Japanese culture? *(Possible responses: I like the games, I like the festivals.)*

REVISIT THE BOOK

READER RESPONSE

1. Japanese: Tamaire, 50 balls.
   Same: 2 teams, basket on a pole.
   American: basketball, 1 ball.
2. Responses will vary.
3. The pattern of a song
4. Possible response: The kimono is more colorful and fancy.

EXTEND UNDERSTANDING Invite students to look through the order of the illustrations. Ask students if they think the photographs could appear in any other order and why.

RESPONSE OPTIONS

WRITING Ask students to write a letter to an imaginary pen pal in Japan. Discuss with students what kinds of questions they might have for their pen pal and what kinds of questions they imagine their pen pal might have for them. Encourage students to include drawings about the United States or pictures they can cut out from old magazines.

SOCIAL STUDIES CONNECTION

Invite students to have their own Children's Day celebration. Draw, paint, or color and then cut out banners in the shape of fish for both boys and girls. Hang in the classroom.

Time For
SOCIAL
STUDIES

Skill Work

TEACH/REVIEW VOCABULARY

Review vocabulary words with students. Then, for the word cotton, ask students, "If you were wearing something made of cotton, what would it feel like?" Personalize all other vocabulary words in this same way.

ELL Go over vocabulary words with English learners, then have them give you each word in a sentence.

TARGET SKILL AND STRATEGY

COMPARE AND CONTRAST Remind students that a *comparison* shows how two or more things are alike. A *contrast* shows how two or more things are different. Explain that clue words such as *like* and *similar* help identify comparisons; clue words *but* and *unlike* show contrasts. Suggest students use a graphic organizer to compare and contrast the United States with Japan as they read *East Meets West: Japan and America*.

PREDICT/CONFIRM PREDICTIONS Remind students that *predicting* means to guess what will happen next based on what they have read already. Ask students to predict what this selection will be about, based on the title, illustrations, and captions. Have students write down details as they read that support or change their prediction. Remind students that making predictions can help them compare and contrast.

ADDITIONAL SKILL INSTRUCTION

GENERALIZE Remind students that a *generalization* is a broad statement or rule that applies to many examples and is made after thinking about what facts have in common. Generalizations often have clue words such as *everyone, many, always, usually, seldom,* and *in general*, and that not all generalizations are valid. Examples: "All animals with fur hibernate," "All robins fly." Discuss whether these generalizations are valid. As students read, ask them to write two generalizations.

Compare and Contrast

- Remember, when you **compare** two or more things, you show the similarities between them.
- When you **contrast** them, you show the differences.

Directions Here are some facts about Japanese and American cultures. Using the graphic organizer, put the facts about Japan under the right heading.

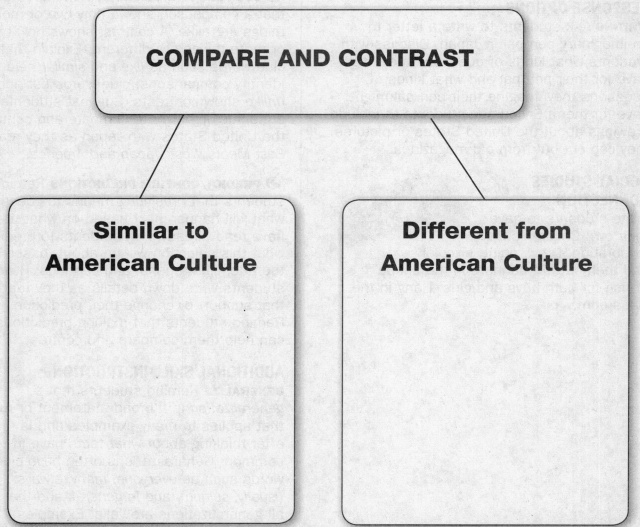

COMPARE AND CONTRAST

Similar to American Culture

Different from American Culture

Vocabulary

Directions On Japanese New Year, families play a game called Karula. Parts of poems are printed on cards. Players match the cards to read the poems out loud. Using the vocabulary words, make up a poem. Then write out the definitions of each word.

Check the Words You Know

___cotton   ___festival   ___graceful   ___handkerchief
___pace   ___pale   ___rhythm   ___snug

Your Poem

_____

_____

_____

_____

_____

_____

_____

Your Definitions

cotton _____

festival _____

graceful _____

handkerchief _____

rhythm _____

pale _____

snug _____

pace _____

The American Dream: Coming to the United States

SUMMARY This reader discusses why immigrants leave their native countries to come to America. It talks about how the history of immigration is woven into the history of this country. Immigrants come to the United States for better jobs and income, better living conditions, and better educational opportunities for their children.

LESSON VOCABULARY

admire	custom
famous	mention
overnight	popular
public	twist

INTRODUCE THE BOOK

INTRODUCE THE TITLE AND AUTHOR Discuss with students the title and author of *The American Dream: Coming to the United States*. Based on the title, ask students what kind of information they think this book will provide. Have students look at the cover photograph to see if they can get additional clues about the book's content.

BUILD BACKGROUND Ask students to talk about where their own family emigrated from, even if it was many years ago. Do they know why their relatives came to the United States? Do they know how they traveled—by boat, airplane, train, or car?

PREVIEW/USE TEXT FEATURES Invite students to look at the illustrations and captions in the book. Ask students how these text features give clues about what is going to be discussed in the text.

READ THE BOOK

SET PURPOSE Have students set a purpose for reading *The American Dream: Coming to the United States*. Students may focus on the reasons immigrants choose for coming to the United States.

STRATEGY SUPPORT: TEXT STRUCTURE In order to help students recognize how the book is organized, have them summarize the information on each page of the book. Afterwards, have them read their summary sentences out loud. Encourage them to explain how summarizing helped them recognize the text structure.

COMPREHENSION QUESTIONS

PAGE 3 What do all Americans have in common? *(They are all immigrants or related to immigrants.)*

PAGE 5 Where did the ancestors of Native Americans come from? *(Asia)*

PAGE 9 Why might American schools be attractive to immigrants? *(Public schools are free and equal.)*

PAGE 10 What freedoms do people come here to find? *(religious and political)*

PAGE 11 Name one famous immigrant mentioned in the book. *(Arnold Schwarzenegger or Patrick Ewing)*

PAGE 12 How different do you think the United States would be without immigrants? *(Possible responses: fewer ethnic restaurants, less diversity)*

REVISIT THE BOOK

READER RESPONSE

1. Possible response: Fact: "Today, about one million people immigrate to the United States every year." Opinion: immigration has made the United States the strong nation that it is today.
2. 1) What immigration means; 2) Why people immigrate; 3) Who some well-known immigrants are
3. twist: to wind together, as in a braid
4. Possible responses: the U.S. flag and the bald eagle

EXTEND UNDERSTANDING Remind students that a *cause* is why something happened and an *effect* is what happened. Ask students to write down the causes for immigration in one column, and then in a separate column, write down the effects.

RESPONSE OPTIONS

WRITING Have students imagine they are immigrants who have just arrived in this country. Have them write a letter to a friend in their home country about what it feels like to be in the United States. Have them describe the reasons why they decided to come to the United States.

SOCIAL STUDIES CONNECTION

Time For SOCIAL STUDIES

Have students research immigration in this country. At different times immigrants come from certain countries. Find out which countries most immigrants are coming from today. From which countries did most immigrants come 100 years ago?

Skill Work

TEACH/REVIEW VOCABULARY

Review the vocabulary words. Then play *Vocabulary Master* with students. Give students three different definitions for each vocabulary word, including one that is silly. Have them select the correct definition and then use the word in a sentence.

ELL Ask English learners to skim the book and write down any unfamiliar words. Suggest that they look the words up in the dictionary and write the meaning in their notebooks.

TARGET SKILL AND STRATEGY

FACT AND OPINION Remind students that a statement of *fact* is a statement that can be proven true or false; a statement of *opinion* is someone's viewpoint. Explain that facts can be proven true or false by checking in books; by observing, weighing, or measuring; or by consulting an expert. Give students several sentences, some of which are statements of fact and some statements of opinion, and have them label each accordingly. Then have students write their own statements of fact and statements of opinion about a topic of their choice.

TEXT STRUCTURE Remind students that authors use different *text structures*. They may organize the information in a book by subject matter; by chronological, or time, order; or in another way. Ask: How does the author organize the information in this book? Challenge students to find statements of fact and statements of opinion in different parts of the book.

ADDITIONAL SKILL INSTRUCTION

DRAW CONCLUSIONS Remind students that *drawing conclusions* means "making a decision that makes sense after thinking about some facts or details." Give students a few sentences about a topic related to this book, and have them draw reasonable conclusions about that topic.

Name _____

Fact and Opinion

When you read nonfiction, you may read some sentences that contain statements of **fact** and others that contain statements of **opinion**. Facts can be proved true or false. Opinions are statements of ideas and feelings. They cannot be proved.

Directions Read the following sentences about *The American Dream: Coming to the United States*. Write whether each one is a fact or an opinion, and explain why.

1. The population of the United States is a blend of people from many countries.

_____

2. Many people believe that immigration has made the United States a strong nation.

_____

3. About one million people immigrate to the United States every year.

_____

4. In the United States they will earn more money to support their families.

_____

5. Living conditions in their home countries are poor.

_____

Directions Read the following paragraph. Then write down two facts and two opinions on the lines below. Then change one of the opinions into a fact.

Some people come to the United States to give their children a better education. Maybe they could not pay to send their children to school in their native countries. Or maybe the schools there were not good. In the United States, public schools promise a free and equal education for all children.

6. _____

7. _____

8. _____

9. _____

10. _____

Vocabulary

Directions Read each sentence. Write the word from the word box that best matches the definition.

Check the Words You Know

___admire	___custom	___famous	___mention
___overnight	___popular	___public	___twist

_____ **1.** *v.* to tell or speak about something

_____ **2.** *n.* a winding together

_____ **3.** *adj.* liked by most people

_____ **4.** *n.* old or usual way of doing things

_____ **5.** *adj.* of or for everyone; belonging to the people

_____ **6.** *adv.* during the night

_____ **7.** *adj.* very well known

_____ **8.** *v.* to look at with approval

Directions Write a paragraph discussing the dreams described in *The American Dream: Coming to the United States,* using as many vocabulary words as possible.

_____

_____

_____

_____

_____

_____

A Child's Life in Korea

SUMMARY A child's life in Korea is similar in many ways to a child's life in the United States. On the other hand, there are also differences. Korean customs, school life, and holidays are all described in this book.

LESSON VOCABULARY

airport	curious
delicious	described
farewell	homesick
memories	raindrops

INTRODUCE THE BOOK

INTRODUCE THE TITLE AND AUTHOR Discuss with students the title and the author of *A Child's Life in Korea*. Ask students to discuss what they think the book will be about based on the title and the cover illustration. Ask whether the social studies content triangle suggests that this is a work of fiction or nonfiction.

BUILD BACKGROUND Invite students to talk about friends who live in other parts of the world. Ask students how their friends' schools are different from or similar to their own school. Ask students about customs in different parts of the world. Ask: What are some holidays that people in other parts of the world celebrate? How are they like or unlike the holidays we celebrate?

PREVIEW Have students preview the book by looking at the illustrations. Ask them to discuss how these text features give an idea of what this book will cover. Ask what they think they will learn from this book.

READ THE BOOK

SET PURPOSE Have students set a purpose for reading *A Child's Life in Korea*. Students' interest in what schools, holidays, and customs are like in other parts of the world should guide this purpose.

STRATEGY SUPPORT: MONITOR AND FIX UP Invite students to use these fix-up strategies if they find they do not understand something in the text. Encourage them to look back for information they have forgotten. Encourage them to read on to see if basic ideas are explained on the next pages. Challenge them to summarize facts and details after they finish reading.

COMPREHENSION QUESTIONS

PAGE 5 How are the lives of children in South Korea and the United States alike? *(They have families, go to school, and celebrate holidays.)*

PAGE 6 What happens every Monday morning in a South Korean school? *(Students gather outside for the morning meeting.)*

PAGE 9 What is a traditional Saturday activity in Korea? *(visiting grandparents)*

PAGE 10 What do Korean students write about in their journals? *(what happens in their lives at school and at home)*

PAGE 11 What is a Korean custom regarding shoes? *("Outside shoes" are left at the door when entering.)*

PAGE 13 According to a Korean tale, what happens if people fall asleep before midnight on Korean New Year? *(Their eyebrows turn white.)*

REVISIT THE BOOK

READER RESPONSE

1. 1) They gather outside the school. 2) The principal talks about doing well. 3) Prizes are given out. 4) Students take off their shoes and enter the school.
2. Possible response: Family is very important to Koreans. Many holidays involve gathering with family members and showing respect to the oldest members.
3. Responses will vary.
4. Responses will vary.

EXTEND UNDERSTANDING Have students comment on the illustrations in the selection. What details about life in Korea can they learn from the illustrations? Invite them to look at the map on page 5. What information can they learn from the map?

RESPONSE OPTIONS

WRITING Invite students to write one paragraph about their favorite holiday. Challenge them to write the sequence of events that happens on that day.

SOCIAL STUDIES CONNECTION

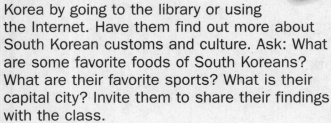

Students can learn more about life in South Korea by going to the library or using the Internet. Have them find out more about South Korean customs and culture. Ask: What are some favorite foods of South Koreans? What are their favorite sports? What is their capital city? Invite them to share their findings with the class.

Skill Work

TEACH/REVIEW VOCABULARY

Invite students to look up each of the vocabulary words and find out how each word is divided into syllables. Invite them to identify the words that are compounds. (raindrops, farewell, airport, homesick)

ELL Write each of the vocabulary words on an index card. Invite students to take turns choosing a card and acting out something to help others guess the word. Continue until all students have had a chance to act for each word.

TARGET SKILL AND STRATEGY

SEQUENCE Remind students that *sequence* is the order of events—what happens first, next, and last. Explain that clue words such as *first, next,* and *last* are not always present. Invite students to look for information from the book that they can arrange in order. Invite them to add clue words to the events to make the sequence clear.

MONITOR AND FIX UP Remind students that good readers check often to make sure they understand what they read. They also recognize when they have stopped understanding and know some fix-up strategies to restore understanding. Challenge students to ask themselves basic questions as they read: What is the author trying to tell readers? What does this mean? Does this make sense? Explain that tracking the sequence of information in the book can help them better understand what they are reading.

ADDITIONAL SKILL INSTRUCTION

AUTHOR'S PURPOSE Remind students that the author's *purpose* is the reason or reasons an author has for writing. Four common purposes are to persuade, to inform, to entertain, and to express. If an author wants to explain some important information, you may want to read more slowly. Challenge students to determine the author's purpose and adjust the way they read accordingly.

Name_____

Sequence

- **Sequence** is the order of events in a story.
- Authors sometimes use clue words such as **first, next, then,** and **last** to tell the order of events.

Directions Read the following paragraph based on *A Child's Life in Korea*. Then put the following events in sequence. Write the letters on the lines below.

> In South Korea, every Monday morning students gather outside for the morning meeting. First the principal talks to the students to encourage them to do well. Next, prizes are awarded to students for good work. Then children take off their outside shoes and put on special shoes they wear only in the classroom. Finally, they go into the classroom to start their day.

a. The children go inside the classroom.

b. Children take off their outside shoes and put on their special shoes.

c. The principal talks to the students.

d. The children gather for the morning meeting.

e. Prizes are awarded to students for good work.

1. _____

2. _____

3. _____

4. _____

5. _____

Name _____

Vocabulary

Directions Match the word parts to make compound words. Draw a line from each word beginning to its ending.

1. home   drops

2. fare   sick

3. rain   port

4. air   well

Directions Read each sentence. Write the word from the word box that best completes each sentence.

5. In the book, the author _____ how Koreans celebrate *Solnal,* or Korean New Year.

6. On New Year's Eve, children try to stay awake until after midnight to say

   _____ to the past year.

7. Wearing traditional Korean clothing brings back _____ of the past.

8. _____ children can read about Korean customs in books.

9. *Chusok* is a two-day harvest festival when Koreans eat much _____ food.

10. Have you ever felt _____ when you were far away from home?

The World of Bread!

SUMMARY This book is all about bread. The author describes the different types of bread that are made in countries across the globe. The author also discusses the history of bread, how bread is made, and how pizza was invented in Italy.

LESSON VOCABULARY

bakery	batch
boils	braided
dough	ingredients
knead	mixture

INTRODUCE THE BOOK

INTRODUCE THE TITLE AND AUTHOR Discuss with students the title and author of *The World of Bread!* Based on the book's title, ask students what kind of information they think this book will provide.

BUILD BACKGROUND Ask students to name as many different kinds of bread as they can think of. Ask them if they have ever made or helped make bread. What was the process? What is their favorite kind of bread? What would the world be like without bread?

PREVIEW/SIDEBARS Have students read all the sidebars in the story. What kinds of information are usually given in sidebars?

ELL Have students describe the type of bread made in their native country. What is the word for *bread* in their native language?

READ THE BOOK

SET PURPOSE Have students set a purpose for reading *The World of Bread!* Have them think about the different kinds of bread they have eaten. Suggest that they take notes as they read on the types of bread that were new to them.

STRATEGY SUPPORT: SUMMARIZE Remind students that in order to draw conclusions accurately, good readers check their understanding of what they read. A good way to do this is to summarize a section, or a whole book. For an article, such as *The World of Bread!*, students should be able to tell the main idea and important details. Suggest rereading parts if students don't understand terms or a section's meaning. Students also may use information from the photographs to help them organize their ideas into a summary.

COMPREHENSION QUESTIONS

PAGE 4 What is unusual about the process of making a bagel? *(It is first boiled, and then it is baked.)*

PAGES 5–6 What do the tortilla and chapati have in common? *(Both are round and flat.)*

PAGE 7 Why is pita bread also called "pocket bread"? *(When cut in half, it forms a pocket that can be filled.)*

PAGE 8 What is the smallest grain in the world? Where is it used to make bread? *(teff, comes from Ethiopia)*

PAGE 9 What is special about challah? *(It is eaten by Jewish people on the Sabbath or holidays; it is braided.)*

PAGE 10 Summarize the story of how pizza was invented. *(A baker in Italy made it as a treat for the queen. He made it on flat bread with the colors of the Italian flag: tomatoes (red), cheese (white), and basil (green).)*

REVISIT THE BOOK

READER RESPONSE

1. It is an important food around the world.
2. Possible response: tortilla, chapati, pita, challah
3. flour, water, dough, poppy seeds, sesame seeds
4. People have been making bread for thousands of years.

EXTEND UNDERSTANDING Have students research how flour is produced. They can use the Internet or library resources to gather information. Is flour produced differently in different countries? Is flour always made out of wheat? How was wheat harvested before harvesting machines were invented?

RESPONSE OPTIONS

WRITING Suggest that students write about a memory they have of making bread, watching a family member make bread, or eating freshly baked bread. Have them describe the sights, tastes, and smells. Or have them describe a memory of a trip to a bakery.

SCIENCE CONNECTIONS

Have students research yeast either on the Internet or in the library. How does yeast make bread rise? What kinds of bread is it possible to make without using yeast? How is yeast produced? When did people start making bread with yeast?

Skill Work

TEACH/REVIEW VOCABULARY

To reinforce the contextual meaning of the word *knead* on page 3, discuss how the phrase "and shapes it into a batch of loaves" gives a clue about the meaning. Do the same exercise for the other vocabulary words.

TARGET SKILL AND STRATEGY

DRAW CONCLUSIONS Remind students that *drawing conclusions* means making a decision that makes sense after thinking about facts or details. Have students think about the following question while they read to see if they can draw any conclusions from the text to answer it: Why are there so many different types of bread in the United States?

SUMMARIZE Remind students that *summarizing* is boiling down a story to its main points. Ask students to summarize a familiar story, such as *Jack and the Beanstalk,* or a familiar movie, such as *Finding Nemo.*

ADDITIONAL SKILL INSTRUCTION

MAIN IDEA Remind students that every story has one or more main ideas. Ask students to take notes as they read, listing the main points and supporting details. Ask students to think about what the main idea of this book is.

Name _____

Draw Conclusions

- To draw a **conclusion** is to think about facts and details and decide something about them.

Directions Read the following passage about chapati. Insert one fact about chapati in each fact box, and then see what conclusion you can draw.

> In India, children eat *chapati*. This is a flat, round, chewy bread. The dough is shaped into a circle and browned on both sides in a very hot frying pan. Then it is held above an open flame for less than a second. This causes the chapati to puff up with steam, like a balloon.

Fact   **Fact**   **Conclusion**

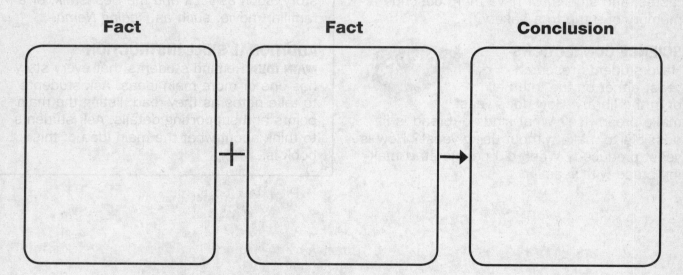

© Pearson Education 3

Name _____

Vocabulary

Directions Complete each sentence with the word from the word box that fits best.

Check the Words You Know

___bakery	___batch	___boils	___braided
___dough	___ingredients	___knead	___mixture

1. Challah, which is eaten in many Jewish homes on the Sabbath, is often

   _____.

2. To make bread, you have to get the right _____ of flour and water.

3. Before bread can be baked, the baker first has to _____ the dough.

4. Before baking bagels, the baker first _____ them.

5. Only the baker knew the proper _____ to make his famous brownies.

6. During Christmas week, the baker always made an extra _____ of Santa Claus cookies.

7. We buy our bread and rolls from a _____.

8. One has to be patient while the _____ is rising.

Directions Write a paragraph about different kinds of bread, using as many vocabulary words as possible.

_____

_____

_____

_____

_____

A Walk Around the City

SUMMARY This nonfiction book shows the many ways people live, work, and play in a city. It focuses on New York City, but it also encourages students to think about their own city and its inhabitants.

LESSON VOCABULARY

cardboard	feast
fierce	flights
pitcher	ruined
stoops	treasure

INTRODUCE THE BOOK

INTRODUCE THE TITLE AND AUTHOR Discuss with students the title and author of *A Walk Around the City*. Ask students what kind of information they think this book will provide based on its title. Ask students to tell whether the scene pictured in the cover photograph is of a small town or a big city. Ask them what clues they used to guess that it's a big city.

BUILD BACKGROUND Discuss with students the various activities in a city. Ask them if they have visited a city other than their own. Ask what they remember about it and the people living there. Ask what they know about cities from television shows, movies, or other books.

PREVIEW/USE TEXT FEATURES Suggest that students skim the heads, photos, and captions in the book. Ask students what clues they used to know this book is about modern-day cities, not those from a century ago.

ELL Ask students to talk about where they used to live. Have them name one difference and one similarity between the place he or she described and the city in the cover photo.

READ THE BOOK

SET PURPOSE Have students set a purpose for reading *A Walk Around the City*. Ask students if they are curious to know about places other than their own city or town. Suggest that they write down notes as they read about any differences between their location and New York City.

STRATEGY SUPPORT: PRIOR KNOWLEDGE Remind students that all cities have some things in common. Suggest that as they read, they think about any personal experiences they have had in a city that are like those discussed in the book. They can also draw on what they have read, heard, or seen about city life. Discuss how using prior knowledge helps readers better understand the author's purpose.

COMPREHENSION QUESTIONS

PAGE 4 Why do you think the author chose to write about New York City? *(She lives there.)*

PAGE 6 Name three ways people use to get around in a city. *(walking, cars, trains, buses, subway)*

PAGE 10 What are two generalizations about cities on this page? Which two words are clue words? *(All cities offer things for people to do for fun. Usually, near the center of a city, you can find museums, zoos, and parks. The clue words are* all *and* usually.*)*

PAGE 12 Can you name another word that means the same thing as *fierce*? Can you think of anything else that you would describe as fierce? *(Possible responses: tough, strong, mean. Tigers and hurricanes can be fierce.)*

REVISIT THE BOOK

READER RESPONSE

1. to inform readers about life in a city
2. Possible responses: Knew: different kinds of buildings, museums; Learned: different city employees, different kinds of commerce
3. the context clue *business*
4. Possible response: The heads are main ideas about the book's topic (cities).

EXTEND UNDERSTANDING Ask students if they have a favorite photograph in the book. Then ask them how the photographs helped them understand the book better. Remind students that captions give more information about the photographs, and can contain details not included in the main text.

RESPONSE OPTIONS

WRITING Ask students to write a paragraph about a trip to a zoo, park, or museum. Suggest that they mention how they got there and why it was fun.

SOCIAL STUDIES CONNECTION

Time For SOCIAL STUDIES

Have students use the library or Internet to find out three details about a city they would like to visit someday. Suggest that they include the population of the city in their notes.

Skill Work

TEACH/REVIEW VOCABULARY

Review the vocabulary words by asking students to define them verbally. Then ask students to use each word in a sentence.

TARGET SKILL AND STRATEGY

AUTHOR'S PURPOSE Remind students that the *author's purpose* is the reason why a writer wrote a particular work. The author's purpose can be to entertain, to persuade, to inform, or to express a mood or feeling. Invite students to discuss why the author wrote *A Walk Around the City*. Then ask students what information they think the author wanted them to learn.

PRIOR KNOWLEDGE Remind students that *prior knowledge* gathered from other books or their personal experiences can help them understand a book and why the author wrote the book. Invite students to create a KWL chart that contains one column each for "What I <u>K</u>now," "What I <u>W</u>ant to Know," and "What I <u>L</u>earned." Prior to reading the book, but after they skim it, ask them to fill in the first and second columns with what they know about cities and what they want to learn. Ask them to fill in the last column after reading the book. Invite students to share their charts with the class.

ADDITIONAL SKILL INSTRUCTION

GENERALIZE Remind students that a *generalization* is a broad statement that applies to many examples. Generalizations often include words such as *many*, *most*, and *generally*. Ask students to use one of these words to write one generalization about what people can do in a city.

Name _____

Author's Purpose

- The **author's purpose** is the reason or reasons an author has for writing a story.
- An author may have one or more reasons for writing.

Directions Read the following passage. Then answer the questions below.

Take a walk around your city. You will see people working in bakeries and in all kinds of stores. Walk past a school and see teachers and librarians at work. See the hospital? Nurses and doctors work there. People work at all kinds of jobs in the city.

1. Why do you think the author wrote this passage?

_____

_____

2. What is another reason the author may have written this passage?

_____

_____

3. Why do you think the author asks the reader to "Take a walk around your city"?

_____

_____

4. Why do you think the author mentions teachers, librarians, doctors, and nurses?

_____

_____

Name _____

Vocabulary

Directions Fill in each blank with the word from the word box that fits best.

Check the Words You Know

| ___cardboard | ___feast | ___fierce | ___flights |
| ___pitcher | ___ruined | ___stoops | ___treasure |

1. When we sat down to lunch, the waiter brought us a _____ of water.

2. The delivery came in a huge _____ box that we used afterwards to build a fort.

3. The highlight of the street fair was a _____ of many different types of food.

4. _____ winds tore the roof off the town hall.

5. A city's most valuable _____ is its people.

6. When the rain came, it _____ our chalk drawings on the sidewalk.

7. Our apartment is up three _____ of stairs.

Directions Write a paragraph about city life that uses several of the vocabulary words.

_____

_____

_____

_____

_____

The Statue of Liberty: From Paris to New York City

SUMMARY This book is about the origins of the Statue of Liberty. It also gives students information about Paris and New York around that time and shows how the countries were friends. Students will also learn how the Statue of Liberty became a symbol for freedom for our society.

LESSON VOCABULARY

crown	liberty
models	symbol
tablet	torch
unforgettable	unveiled

INTRODUCE THE BOOK

INTRODUCE THE TITLE AND AUTHOR Discuss with students the title and the author of *The Statue of Liberty: From Paris to New York City*. Ask students if the title and the photograph on the cover give them any clues as to what this selection is about.

BUILD BACKGROUND Ask students what they know about the Statue of Liberty and if they have ever been to the Statue of Liberty or seen pictures about it. Discuss with students what freedom means to them.

ELL Invite students to talk about important statues in their native countries. Suggest they bring in photographs if they have them, or draw a picture of one of the statues.

PREVIEW/USE TEXT FEATURES Invite students to look at the photographs, captions, and labels in this book. Discuss how each of these text elements gives students a glimpse into what life must have been like in the 1880s in Paris and New York.

READ THE BOOK

SET PURPOSE Have students set a purpose for reading *The Statue of Liberty: From Paris to New York City*. Students' curiosity about great monuments or about Paris or New York should guide this purpose, but the photographs from the 1800s should also prove fascinating.

STRATEGY SUPPORT: TEXT STRUCTURE Explain that there are several ways to organize a text—for example, sequence of events, comparison and contrast, description, or definition. Because the text provides facts and characteristics, readers come to understand the main idea through paying attention to the descriptions and sensory details.

COMPREHENSION QUESTIONS

PAGE 3 What two things did the Statue of Liberty symbolize? *(friendship between France and the United States; freedom)*

PAGE 4 What does the map on page 4 tell you about the city of Paris? *(Possible responses: many roads; the river Seine runs through center of Paris; busy and crowded; a right bank and a left bank)*

PAGE 6 Why do you think Bartholdi made models of every part of the Statue of Liberty before he built it? *(Possible response: Building a small model can save time by giving an idea of what it will look like when large.)*

PAGE 9 What is the main idea on this page? *(New York in the 1880s was full of amazing sights, including the Brooklyn Bridge.)*

PAGE 10 What two text features show you two sides of New York in the 1880s? *(A photograph of immigrants crowded in the city and a photo of a mansion show New York with poor and rich people.)*

REVISIT THE BOOK

READER RESPONSE

1. Paris in the 1880s was a very old and beautiful city.

2. Left circle: Seine, Right Bank, Left Bank, Cathedral of Notre Dame, Arc de Triomphe Right circle: Lights, first to get electricity, Brooklyn Bridge, Central Park, crowded Center circle: friendship, gift of Statue of Liberty, big city, crowded, old and new

3. *Unforgettable*: not able to forget. *Forgettable*: able to be forgotten. *Unpacked*: took out of a crate, box, or case. *Packed*: put into a crate, box, or case. *Unveiled*: took off a covering. *Veiled*: covered.

4. Responses will vary.

EXTEND UNDERSTANDING Discuss with students how descriptive words can help you visualize and so better understand what you are reading. Invite students to make a graphic organizer with the headings *Paris* and *New York*. Suggest that students list all the word pictures of Paris and of New York that they find in this book, and that they can also add any descriptive words of their own into this organizer.

RESPONSE OPTIONS

WRITING Suggest students imagine that they are the Statue of Liberty and have them write about what it was like to look at New York City from your island in New York Harbor.

SOCIAL STUDIES CONNECTION

Suggest students do more research on why the Statue of Liberty is a symbol of freedom. Invite students to make up and draw their own symbols of freedom. Post around the classroom.

Time For SOCIAL STUDIES

Skill Work

TEACH/REVIEW VOCABULARY

Review vocabulary words with students. Then, write down a list of definitions in one row and the list of vocabulary words in another and have students match the words to the correct definitions.

TARGET SKILL AND STRATEGY

MAIN IDEA Remind students that the *main idea* is the most important idea about the topic. Model a way of determining the main idea of this book by asking these questions: What is this book about in a few words? *(the Statue of Liberty)* What is the most important idea about this topic? *(The statue was offered as a symbol of friendship and took several years to complete.)*

TEXT STRUCTURE Remind students that a way to find the main idea is to recognize the *text structure* that shows how the book is organized. Call attention to the heads, photographs, and captions. These elements help students gain significant information, and understand more about the times when the statue was created.

ADDITIONAL SKILL INSTRUCTION

FACT AND OPINION Remind students that a *statement of fact* is something that can be proven true or false, and a *statement of opinion* expresses ideas or feelings. Invite students to list facts they read about New York, Paris, and the Statue of Liberty in this book. Then ask them to list any opinions they might find in the book. Suggest that as they read, students can add more facts and opinions to their list.

Main Idea

- The **main idea** is the most important idea about the topic.
- Sometimes the main idea is stated in a sentence, but when it isn't, you have to figure it out and state it in your own words.

Directions Read the following passages from the story *The Statue of Liberty: From Paris to New York City.* Circle the correct main idea in each.

1. What was New York City like in 1886? At night the city was ablaze with light. New York City was the first city in the world lighted by electricity!
   a. New York City was a busy city.
   b. New York in 1886 was full of light.
   c. New York City was the first city to have electricity.

2. The Statue of Liberty was being unveiled. Thousands of New Yorkers watched the unforgettable sight from the shores of Manhattan.
   a. Thousands of New Yorkers came to the shores.
   b. The Statue of Liberty was unveiled.
   c. People like to see new statues.

3. The Paris of today still has much of the charm of the old city. But not everything in Paris is old. There are new parks and gardens. You can ride down wide, tree-lined avenues where you will see new railroad stations, government buildings, and theaters.
   a. Paris has many parks and gardens.
   b. Paris today is a mixture of old and new.
   c. You can have a lot of fun in Paris.

Directions Look at the main ideas written below. Can you think of a supporting detail for each idea? For example, if the main idea is "Bob loves to sing," a supporting detail might be "and he is always giving musical concerts." Try it yourself!

4. My dog Skip loves the park. _____

_____

5. Keeping your teeth clean is important. _____

_____

© Pearson Education 3

Vocabulary

Directions Fill in the missing letters for each vocabulary word. Then use the word in a sentence.

Check the Words You Know

___crown   ___liberty   ___models   ___symbol
___tablet   ___torch   ___unforgettable   ___unveiled

1. __r__wn _____

_____

2. __ __b__ __ty _____

_____

3. t__ __ch _____

_____

4. __ __for__et__able _____

_____

5. m__de__s _____

_____

6. __ __mbol _____

_____

7. t__ __let _____

_____

8. un__ei__ed _____

_____

The Sights and Sounds of New York City's Chinatown

SUMMARY This book describes New York City's Chinatown. It describes the people who live there, as well as the sights, sounds, and traditions of this colorful and lively neighborhood. It discusses several important celebrations, like the Chinese New Year. It even gives a recipe for moon cakes.

LESSON VOCABULARY

bows	chilly	foolish
foreign	narrow	perches
recipe		

INTRODUCE THE BOOK

INTRODUCE THE TITLE AND AUTHOR Introduce students to the title and the author of the book *The Sights and Sounds of New York City's Chinatown*. Ask students what they think this book will be about, based on the title. Does the cover of the book offer any clues? Can they imagine what some of the sights and sounds of Chinatown might be?

BUILD BACKGROUND Discuss with students what they know about Chinatown. Ask them whether they have ever visited Chinatown in New York or another city. What do they remember about their visit? What surprised them the most? What are their favorite types of Chinese food? Have they ever eaten with chopsticks?

PREVIEW/USE PHOTOS AND CAPTIONS Invite students to look through the photographs, charts, and captions in the book. Ask the students what they think the text could be about now that they have taken a look at the pictures.

ELL Ask if any students have ever been to a Chinatown, whether in New York or elsewhere. Have them describe one thing they remember seeing or hearing while there. If you have any students from China, have them describe what they enjoy about Chinese New Year or discuss another custom such as eating with chopsticks.

READ THE BOOK

SET PURPOSE Most students will be interested in reading this book so that they can learn about Chinatown, a special neighborhood in New York City. Remind students that interest in other cultures is an important attitude to have.

STRATEGY SUPPORT: GRAPHIC ORGANIZERS We use this skill typically before, during, and after reading, and to assess what we've read. With this book, you may want to focus on the chart on page 8. Talk with students about how this kind of chart helps them organize the ideas they have read.

COMPREHENSION QUESTIONS

PAGE 5 Are the streets of Chinatown wide and straight? *(No, they are short, winding, and narrow.)*

PAGE 7 What languages do you think you might hear walking through Chinatown? *(Chinese and English)*

PAGE 8 Why do many Chinese people like to practice the art of Tai Chi? *(to exercise their minds and bodies)*

PAGE 12 Does the Chinese New Year happen on the same date as traditional American New Year? *(No, it happens sometime in January or February.)*

REVISIT THE BOOK

READER RESPONSE

1. Streets are crowded and busy; important Chinese traditions are falling away; there are many choices of food and other products.
2. Sights: narrow winding streets; crowds of Chinese people and tourists; food markets; seasonal festivals
   Sounds: spoken Chinese; traffic noises; music from seasonal festivals
3. chilly, narrow, crowded, loud, noisy, colorful
4. Answers will vary but may include speaking politely and listening when someone is speaking to you.

EXTEND UNDERSTANDING Ask students: Why did the photographs help you picture Chinatown much more clearly than if they were illustrations? What is it about a photograph that makes you feel like you are right there in the middle of the action?

RESPONSE OPTIONS

WRITING Have students imagine that they are attending the New Year's parade in Chinatown. Have them describe the sights, sounds, and smells. Describe the noises of the firecrackers and the fireworks. What kinds of music do they hear? What kinds of people line the streets to watch the parade? Have students write about how it feels to be at the parade.

SOCIAL STUDIES CONNECTION

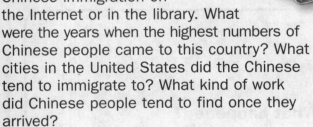

Have students research Chinese immigration on the Internet or in the library. What were the years when the highest numbers of Chinese people came to this country? What cities in the United States did the Chinese tend to immigrate to? What kind of work did Chinese people tend to find once they arrived?

Skill Work

TEACH/REVIEW VOCABULARY

Encourage student pairs to find the vocabulary words in the text. Have them define the words and then work together to write a sentence for each word.

TARGET SKILL AND STRATEGY

CAUSE AND EFFECT Remind students that an *effect* is what happened and a *cause* is why something happened. Have students read page 8. Ask: Name one reason why the older generation feels that their traditions are slipping away. *(Younger Chinese do not bow to their elders.)* Or ask: Name one reason why Chinese people don't celebrate individual birthdays. *(They just add a year each New Year.)*

GRAPHIC ORGANIZERS Remind students that *graphic organizers* are a visual way to arrange information. Have students look at the table on page 8. Help them explore the reasons (right-hand column) for three Chinese traditions (left-hand column).

ADDITIONAL SKILL INSTRUCTION

GENERALIZE Remind students that a *generalization* is a broad statement or rule that applies to many examples. Have students compare a traditional American New Year with the Chinese New Year celebration described in the book. What are some of the similarities? *(parades, fireworks, noise, crowds)*

Cause and Effect

- A **cause** is *why* something happened.
- An **effect** is *what* happened.

Directions For each cause, write an effect. Use *The Sights and Sounds of New York City's Chinatown* to help you. The same cause may have different effects.

Causes	Effects
1. Many Chinatown residents come from China. **Why did it happen?**	→ **What happened?**
2. Many Chinatown residents come from China. **Why did it happen?**	→ **What happened?**
3. Many young Chinatown residents do not show respect to their elders. **Why did it happen?**	→ **What happened?**
4. Many Chinatown residents want to exercise their minds and bodies. **Why did it happen?**	→ **What happened?**
5. Some people want to avoid the crowds at the Chinese New Year celebrations. **Why did it happen?**	→ **What happened?**

Vocabulary

Directions Fill in the blank with the word from the box that matches the definition.

```
Check the Words You Know

___ bows          ___ chilly
___ foolish       ___ foreign
___ narrow        ___ perches
___ recipe
```

1. _____ from a country other than your own

2. _____ places to view things from high above

3. _____ leans forward to show respect

4. _____ silly; not wise

5. _____ instructions for cooking

6. _____ having a small width; not very wide

7. _____ slightly cold

Directions Write a paragraph about Chinatown as described in *The Sights and Sounds of New York City's Chinatown*. Use at least three vocabulary words.

_____

_____

_____

_____

_____

_____

_____

A Different Drawing

SUMMARY In this story, a girl is encouraged to draw what she feels, instead of conforming to the expectations of her classmates. It supports the lesson concept of freedom of expression in a free society.

LESSON VOCABULARY

encourages	expression
local	native
settled	social
support	

INTRODUCE THE BOOK

INTRODUCE THE TITLE AND AUTHOR Discuss with students the title and the author of *A Different Drawing*. Also have students look at the picture on the cover. Explain to students that social studies is the study of how people live as a group. Ask: How might this story have something to do with social studies?

BUILD BACKGROUND Ask students to name their favorite book, and lead them in a short discussion about the differences among the books. Then say: Suppose a law said that everyone had to read the same kind of book. Would that be okay with you? Why or why not?

PREVIEW/USE ILLUSTRATIONS Have students look at the pictures in the book before reading. Ask: Who is the story about? Where does the story happen? Have students read the heading on page 16. Discuss with students whether this page is part of the story.

READ THE BOOK

SET PURPOSE Have students set a purpose for reading *A Different Drawing*. Students may need help setting their own purposes. Ask: Do you want to know why the girl is drawing by herself?

STRATEGY SUPPORT: MONITOR AND FIX UP Tell students that one way to monitor, or check, their understanding of a story is to ask questions, such as: Who is the story about? Where does the story happen? When does it happen? What happens in the beginning of the story? in the middle? at the end? Remind students that if they can't answer the questions, they can reread, adjust their reading rate, or seek help. Suggest that students practice by writing and trying to answer questions about selected passages.

ELL Students may have difficulty with the words *mural* and *wavy* (page 3), *lollipops* (page 4), and *octopus* and *monkey* (page 11). For each of these terms, draw representative pictures and have students label them in both English and their home languages.

COMPREHENSION QUESTIONS

PAGE 3 How are the children in Sue's class alike? *(They want to know how to draw trees.)*

PAGES 3–7 How do the children try to solve the big problem? *(First Sue offers to help. Then Nat shows how to make lollipop trees.)*

PAGES 10–11 Why do you think Sue wants to draw a tree that looks like an octopus and one that looks like a monkey? *(Possible response: Sue enjoys drawing.)*

PAGE 12 Read what Amy says. Is it a statement of fact or a statement of opinion? Why? *(It is a statement of opinion. Possible response: It can't be proved true or false, because some people might not feel like Amy.)*

REVISIT THE BOOK

READER RESPONSE

1. Possible responses: Fact: *These are local trees. Some are native, and some were planted by the people who settled here.* Opinion: *You are the best artist! That is a wonderful tree!*

2. Responses will vary.

3. grows naturally in a certain place

4. He explained that sometimes kids want to do what is easiest, and sometimes they want to do the same things that other kids do.

EXTEND UNDERSTANDING Ask students to think about the characters in this story. Have them make a Venn diagram to compare and contrast two of the characters. Students should fill in the diagram by writing words that represent the similarities and differences between the two characters.

RESPONSE OPTIONS

WRITING Have students review the background information on page 16. Encourage students to express themselves freely by writing a letter to the editor supporting or opposing Nat's opinion in the story.

SOCIAL STUDIES CONNECTION

Time For
SOCIAL
STUDIES

Have students look up the First Amendment to the U.S. Constitution. Have them list the freedoms it protects. Lead the class in a discussion of these basic rights.

Skill Work

TEACH/REVIEW VOCABULARY

Discuss this week's lesson vocabulary with students. Reinforce word meaning by asking students to complete sentences for each vocabulary word. For example: A person who helps is a person who _____.

TARGET SKILL AND STRATEGY

FACT AND OPINION Remind students that a *statement of fact* tells something that can be proved true or false. A *statement of opinion* tells ideas or feelings. It cannot be proved true or false. Turn to page 5 and read the sentence: "They grow all around the state." Ask: Can you prove this statement true or false? How? Point out this statement on page 4: "Well, you got it *wrong.*" Ask: Is this a statement of fact or a statement of opinion? *(It is Nat's opinion.)*

MONITOR AND FIX UP Tell students to check their understanding as they read by asking questions, such as: Who is the story about? They can also ask questions about statements of fact and statements of opinion; for example: Can this statement be proved true or false?

ADDITIONAL SKILL INSTRUCTION

GENERALIZE Remind students that sometimes when you read, you are given ideas about several things or people and you can make a statement about them all together. This might be how they are mostly alike or all alike in some way. After page 7, ask: How are the other children different from Sue? *(They all wanted to draw green lollipops instead of realistic trees.)*

Fact and Opinion

- A statement of **fact** is a statement that can be proved true or false.
- A statement of **opinion** is a statement of someone's judgment, belief, or way of thinking about something.

Directions Write *F* beside statements of fact and *O* beside statements of opinion.

1. _____ Trees have leaves and branches.

2. _____ There is only one way that you should draw a tree.

3. _____ Sue's trees were better than the other kids' trees.

4. _____ Mr. Martinez encouraged his students to do their best.

5. _____ You should do what other kids tell you to do.

6. _____ There are all sorts of trees.

7. _____ All trees should not look like lollipops.

8. _____ Freedom of expression means that we can express ourselves in many different ways.

Directions Read the statement: Sue's drawings are better than everyone else's drawings. Is this a fact or an opinion? Why?

9–10. _____

_____

_____

_____

_____

Vocabulary

Directions Write the word that best completes each sentence.

Check the Words You Know
___encourages ___expression ___local ___native
___settled ___social ___support

1. A great painting can be an _____ of joy.

2. I was born and raised in this town. I am a _____.

3. They discussed the problem and _____ it by coming to an agreement.

4. Sue _____ the other kids to draw the trees any way they like.

5. Nat talked to many kids. He is very _____.

6. Sue went to the _____ art supply store to buy markers.

7. Mr. Martinez will _____ you, no matter how you draw a tree.

Directions Use the words *local*, *support*, and *expression* in a short paragraph.

_____

_____

_____

_____

_____

_____

Leo and the School of Fish

SUMMARY Leo is a young fish who is tired of always swimming in a school of fish. One day he discovers a shipwreck and swims off alone to explore it. In the wreck, he encounters several dangerous situations, so he decides to return to the safety of his school.

LESSON VOCABULARY

crystal	disappeared
discovery	goal
journey	joyful
scoop	unaware

INTRODUCE THE BOOK

INTRODUCE THE TITLE AND AUTHOR Discuss with students the title and the author of *Leo and the School of Fish.* Ask students what they think the story might be about, based on the title. Have them look at the illustration on the front cover. Does this picture give them any more clues as to what will happen in the story?

BUILD BACKGROUND Ask students what they know about fish and the ocean. Have them describe any trips they've taken to an aquarium. Have them describe any movies they've seen that have shown fish swimming in schools.

ELL Have students describe a trip to the ocean. Have they ever gone fishing in the ocean? Have they ever been to an aquarium? Have them talk about any of these experiences.

PREVIEW/USE ILLUSTRATIONS Invite students to look at all the illustrations in the book. Ask students how the illustrations give clues as to the meaning of the story.

READ THE BOOK

SET PURPOSE Have students set a purpose for reading *Leo and the School of Fish.* Have them follow the plot closely by taking notes as they read.

STRATEGY SUPPORT: VISUALIZE Remind students how to visualize: As you read, form pictures in your mind about what is happening in the story. Tell students that they should combine what they already know with details from the text to create pictures in their minds. Add that they can use all of their senses, not just sight, to help them form pictures. Model: On page 3, I see that Leo is a fish who lives in the sea. I know what the sea is like. I picture that it is cold and wet but very colorful. There are many sea creatures, and some are dangerous. I think it might be fun to swim with the fish.

COMPREHENSION QUESTIONS

PAGE 4 What does Leo's friend Gil think about swimming in a school? *(that it's cool)*

PAGE 6 What does Gil say to Leo about the ship? *(that it could be dangerous, that he might get eaten)*

PAGE 9 What is the first danger Leo finds on the ship? *(a lantern fish with its mouth open)*

PAGE 11 What kind of a fish does Leo find lurking in the corner? *(a huge moray eel that wants to eat him)*

PAGE 13 What happens to Leo as he is fleeing the shipwreck? *(A net comes down around him, but he is able to swim through the holes in the net.)*

PAGE 14 Where does Leo go when he just needs a safe place to think? *(behind some coral)*

REVISIT THE BOOK

READER RESPONSE

1. Possible response: Beginning: Leo is bored of always swimming in his school. Middle: Leo swims into an old ship and encounters dangers. End: Leo returns to the safety of his school.
2. Possible responses should include colorful verbs, adjectives, and adverbs.
3. Responses will vary.
4. Possible response: Advantages of doing things in a group include enjoying safety in numbers, getting help when you need it, and learning from each other. Advantages of doing things alone are that you don't have to compromise, and you can do whatever you want.

EXTEND UNDERSTANDING Have students think about what elements of this story make it a fantasy. Have them list details from the story that describe things that could not really happen.

RESPONSE OPTIONS

WRITING Have students imagine that they are a fish swimming in a large school of fish. Rather than going off on their own, like Leo, students should imagine that they stay with the group all day. Ask students: What is it like to swim in a school? What did you see during the day? How does staying in a large group allow you to be safer from larger creatures who might want to eat you?

SCIENCE CONNECTION

TIME FOR Science

Have students research fish schools. Assign each student a different type of fish. They can use the Internet or the library. Have them draw pictures of their fish. Once they have gathered all their information, have them share it with the class.

Skill Work

TEACH/REVIEW VOCABULARY

Encourage student pairs to find the vocabulary words in the text. Have them define the words and then work together to write a sentence for each word.

TARGET SKILL AND STRATEGY

PLOT AND THEME Remind students that the *plot* is the sequence of events that take a story from the beginning to the middle to the end. Also, remind students that stories usually have one big idea or *theme.* Discuss with students what they think the big idea is in a familiar story like *The Tortoise and the Hare* (slow and steady wins the race). Have them tell the plot of the story by recalling the events in sequence.

VISUALIZE Remind students that when we *visualize,* we form pictures in our minds about what is happening in the story. Encourage students to try to visualize the scenes and characters in *Leo and the School of Fish* as they read it. Have them try to activate all their senses: sight, smell, taste, touch, and hearing.

ADDITIONAL SKILL INSTRUCTION

REALISM AND FANTASY Remind students that a *realistic story* tells about something that could happen, while a *fantasy* is a story about something that could not happen. As they read this story, have them think about what elements of the story are realistic, and which are fantasy.

Plot and Theme

- The **plot** is an organized pattern of events.
- The **theme** is the "big idea" of a story.

Directions Fill in the graphic organizer about the story elements in
Leo and the School of Fish.

Title _____

This story is about _____

_____
(name the characters)

This story takes place _____

_____
(where and when)

The action begins when _____

_____

Then, _____

_____

Next, _____

_____

After that, _____

_____

The story ends when _____

_____

Theme: _____

Vocabulary

Directions Fill in the blank with the word from the box that fits best.

Check the Words You Know

___crystal   ___disappeared   ___discovery   ___goal
___journey   ___joyful   ___scoop   ___unaware

1. Leo didn't listen to his friend Gil and set off on his _____.

2. The fisherman tried to _____ the fish out of the water with the net.

3. The flashing _____ caught Leo's eye.

4. Leo was hoping to make an exciting _____ on his adventure.

5. The fish in the school were _____ when Leo returned safely.

6. Leo swam so fast it looked as if he _____.

7. Leo's _____ was to explore the ship.

8. Leo was _____ of what would happen on his journey.

Directions Write a brief paragraph discussing Leo's journey, using as many vocabulary words as possible.

_____

_____

_____

_____

_____

_____

_____

_____

Glass Blowing

SUMMARY Readers explore the history and methods of making things out of glass. Detailed illustrations and photographs support the concepts in the text. Readers can make predictions, compare methods, and make generalizations about the art of glass blowing.

LESSON VOCABULARY

burros	bursts	factory
glassblower	puff	reply
tune		

INTRODUCE THE BOOK

INTRODUCE THE TITLE AND AUTHOR Discuss with students the title and the author of *Glass Blowing*. Encourage students to comment on how the photo on the cover relates to the title. Ask students to predict what social studies topics may be discussed in this book.

BUILD BACKGROUND Discuss with students the unique characteristics of glass. It is able to withstand heat; it is easy to clean; it is smooth; it can be clear or opaque; it can be made into many shapes large and small.

PREVIEW/USE TEXT FEATURES As students look through the headings, photographs, and illustrations, ask them to comment on things they find surprising. Many students will be surprised by the illustrations on pages 4 and 5 that show glass objects made in ancient times. Others will be surprised by the photographs on pages 8 and 9 that show the temperatures and equipment required to work with glass.

READ THE BOOK

SET PURPOSE Although glass is a very familiar material to students, the way it is made is probably very new to them. Help students read for meaning by suggesting they think of a glass object they use often or particularly like and read to learn how it was made.

STRATEGY SUPPORT: PREDICT Practice this skill after students have read page 12. Remind students that pausing while reading to *predict* what will happen next is a good way to self-check comprehension. Ask students to think about the heading at the top of page 13 and what they have read to predict what the next section will be about. Record their predictions. After students have read page 15, discuss which predictions were correct or incorrect and why.

COMPREHENSION QUESTIONS

PAGE 3 What does the author mean by comparing glass to gold? *(At one time in the past, glass was rare and highly valued, like gold.)*

PAGE 8 What is the first step of glass blowing? *(melting the ingredients)*

PAGE 13 What is the natural color of glass? *(green or greenish-blue)*

PAGE 15 What are some things that glass is used for? *(Possible responses: TV screens, drinking glasses, test tubes)*

REVISIT THE BOOK

READER RESPONSE

1. Responses will vary.
2. Possible response: Glass is recyclable so glass containers may be used more than plastic.
3. Possible response: If glass blowers puff too hard, the bubbles will burst.
4. make the glass, gather it, blow a bubble, shape it, cool it in a special oven

EXTEND UNDERSTANDING To help students understand the differences between the Egyptian method of making glass and glass blowing, have them compare the illustrations on pages 6–12. Encourage students to draw conclusions and make inferences from the graphic sources. Ask: Why do you think the Egyptian method is very slow? Which method would allow you to make a greater variety of shapes with glass? What do you think the mold was made of? Why does it take two people to blow glass?

RESPONSE OPTIONS

WRITING Reinforce students' understanding of the sequence of events in the book by asking them to create a time line about the history of glass.

SOCIAL STUDIES CONNECTION

Time For SOCIAL STUDIES

Arrange with your librarian to have additional books or videos on glass blowing for students to browse after reading. A video of glass blowers would be especially helpful in clarifying students' understanding of the process. Suggest that when they see an object they find interesting, they think about how it was made.

Skill Work

TEACH/REVIEW VOCABULARY

Play Memory. Write these vocabulary words and their synonyms on separate index cards: *burro—donkey; puff—breathe; tune—adjust; factory—plant; burst—blast; reply—answer.* Place the cards word-side down. Students then take turns turning over two cards at a time. Students earn points by turning over and recognizing words with the same meaning.

ELL Play Synonym Memory with a word and matching picture on one side of each card. Adding a picture will help students to recognize synonyms.

TARGET SKILL AND STRATEGY

GENERALIZE Explain: When you read about several people, things, or ideas that are alike, you can make a *generalization* about them. Read the first sentence on page 14. Point out the clue word *much,* which signals a generalization. Group students in pairs and assign each pair a page of text. Have pairs write a generalization based on facts on their page. As a class, evaluate the generalizations by looking at facts in the text.

PREDICT Guide students to look for details that will help them *predict* what will be next. Stop and practice this skill after students have read page 6. Write students' predictions on the board. Then have students read on. As predictions are confirmed as correct or incorrect, pause and encourage class discussion. Explain that making predictions can also help students make generalizations.

ADDITIONAL SKILL INSTRUCTION

COMPARE AND CONTRAST When students come to pages 6 and 7, practice the skill *compare and contrast.* Draw a Venn diagram and complete it as a group. Ask: How are the two ways of making glass alike? How are they different? Next to the Venn diagram write a list of clue words that helped students identify the similarities and differences between the methods.

Name _____

Generalize

- To **generalize** is to make a broad statement or rule that applies to many examples.
- When you make a generalization, you look for similarities or differences among facts and examples in the text.

Directions Complete the graphic organizer below. Find facts from the text that support the generalization.

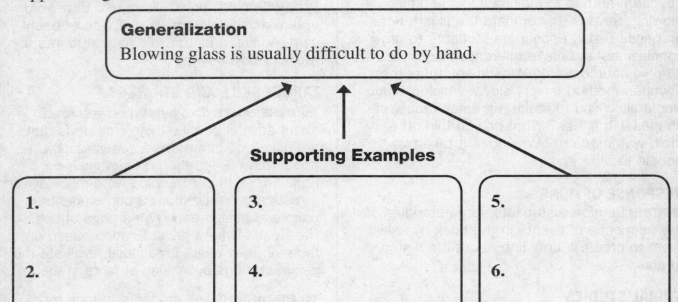

Generalization
Blowing glass is usually difficult to do by hand.

Supporting Examples

1.

2.

3.

4.

5.

6.

Directions Write a generalization about glass factories. Then write three facts that support the generalization.

7. Generalization:

_____

_____

8–10. Supporting examples:

_____

_____

Name _____

Vocabulary

Directions First unscramble each word. Then use the word in a sentence.

```
┌─────────────────────────────────────────────┐
│        Check the Words You Know              │
│  ┌───────────────────────────────────────┐  │
│  │  ___ burros       ___ bursts          │  │
│  │  ___ factory      ___ glassblower     │  │
│  │  ___ puff         ___ reply           │  │
│  │  ___ tune                             │  │
│  └───────────────────────────────────────┘  │
└─────────────────────────────────────────────┘
```

1. etnu _____

_____

2. tbsru _____

_____

3. fufp _____

_____

4. yrfaotc _____

_____

5. orbusr _____

_____

6. ypelr _____

_____

7. bssalgrewol _____

_____

Story Prediction from Previewing

Title _____

Read the title and look at the pictures in the story.
What do you think a problem in the story might be?

I think a problem might be _____

_____

_____

After reading _____ ,
draw a picture of one of the problems in the story.

Story Prediction from Vocabulary

Title and Vocabulary Words

Read the title and the vocabulary words.
What do you think this story might be about?

I think this story might be about _____

_____

_____

After reading _____ ,
draw a picture that shows what the story is about.

KWL Chart

Topic _____

What We **K** now	What We **W** ant to Know	What We **L** earned

Vocabulary Frame

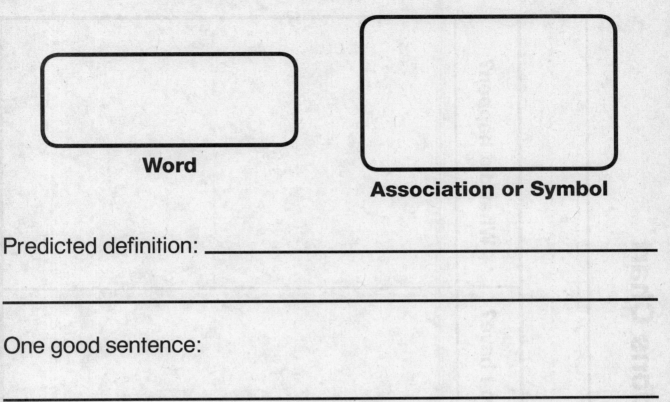

Word

Association or Symbol

Predicted definition: _____

_____

One good sentence:

_____

_____

Verified definition: _____

_____

_____

Another good sentence:

_____

_____

Story Predictions Chart

Title _____

What might happen?	What clues do I have?	What did happen?

Story Sequence A

Title _____

Beginning

Middle

End

Story Sequence B

Title	
Characters	**Setting**

Events

1. First

2. Next

3. Then

4. Last

Story Sequence C

Title

Characters

Problem

Events

_____

_____

_____

_____

_____

_____

_____

_____

Solution

Question the Author

Title _____

Author _____ **Page** _____

I. What does the author tell you?	
2. Why do you think the author tells you that?	
3. Does the author say it clearly?	
4. What would make it clearer?	
5. How would you say it instead?	

Story Comparison

Title A _____

_____

Characters

Setting

Events

Title B _____

_____

Characters

Setting

Events

Web

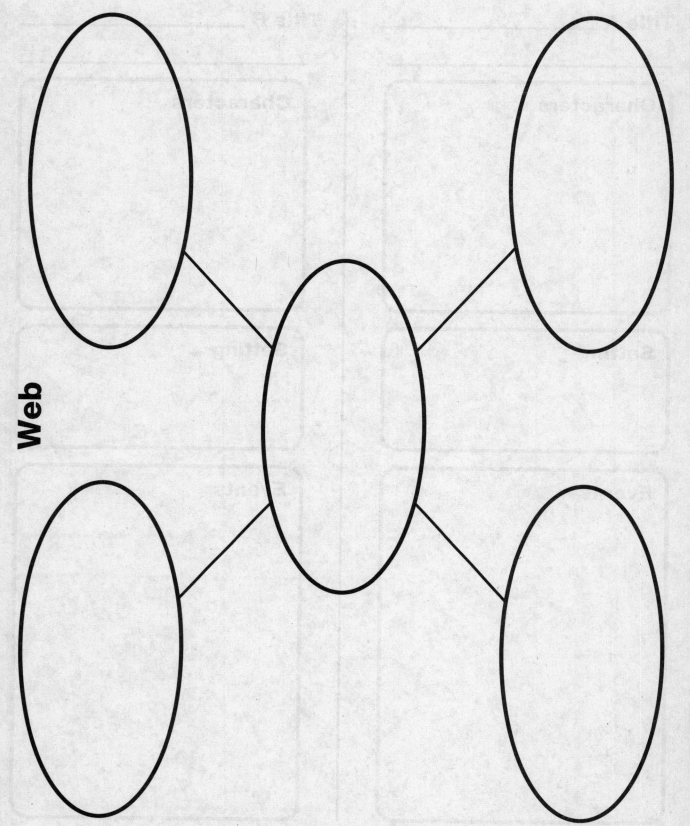

Main Idea

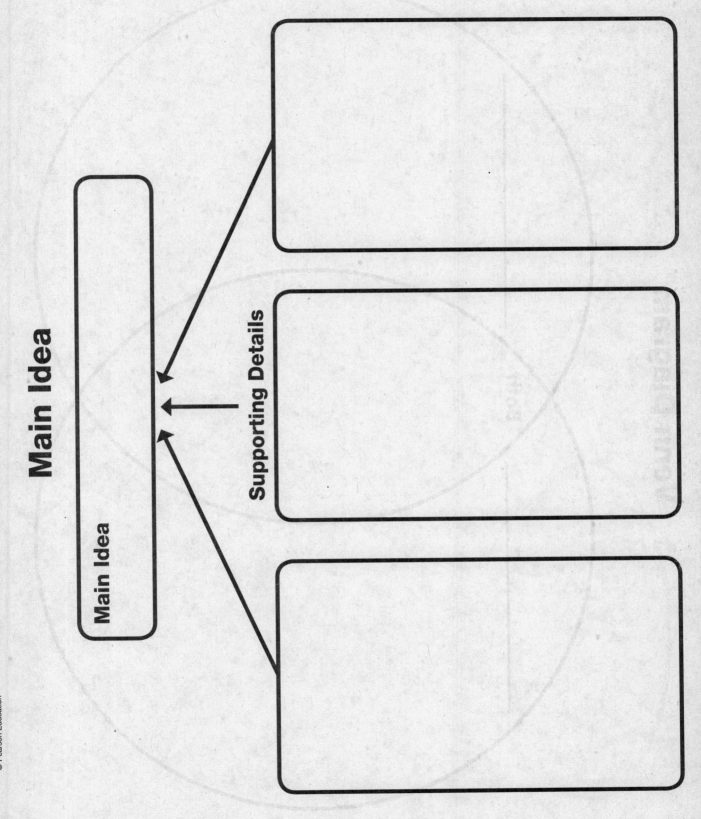

Main Idea

Supporting Details

Venn Diagram

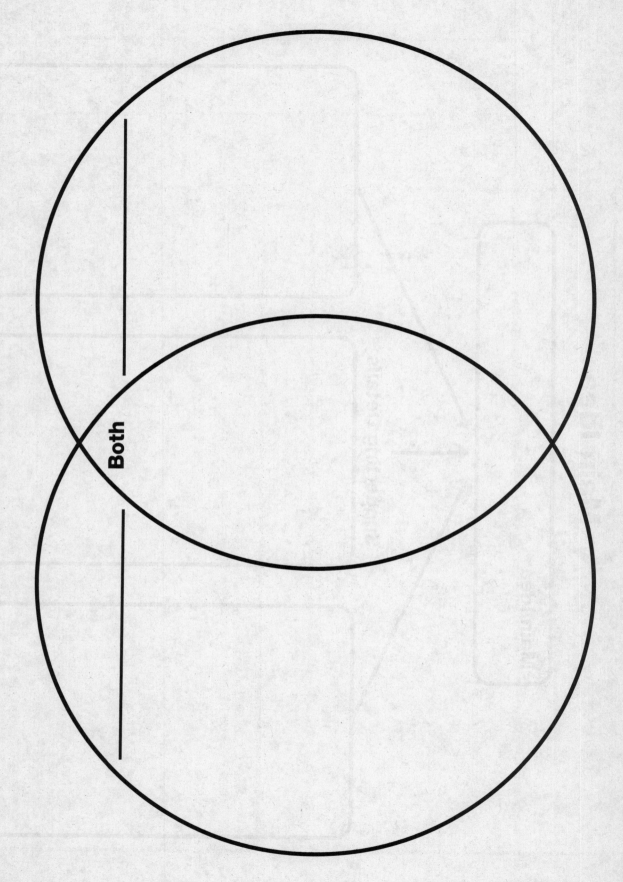

Both

Compare and Contrast

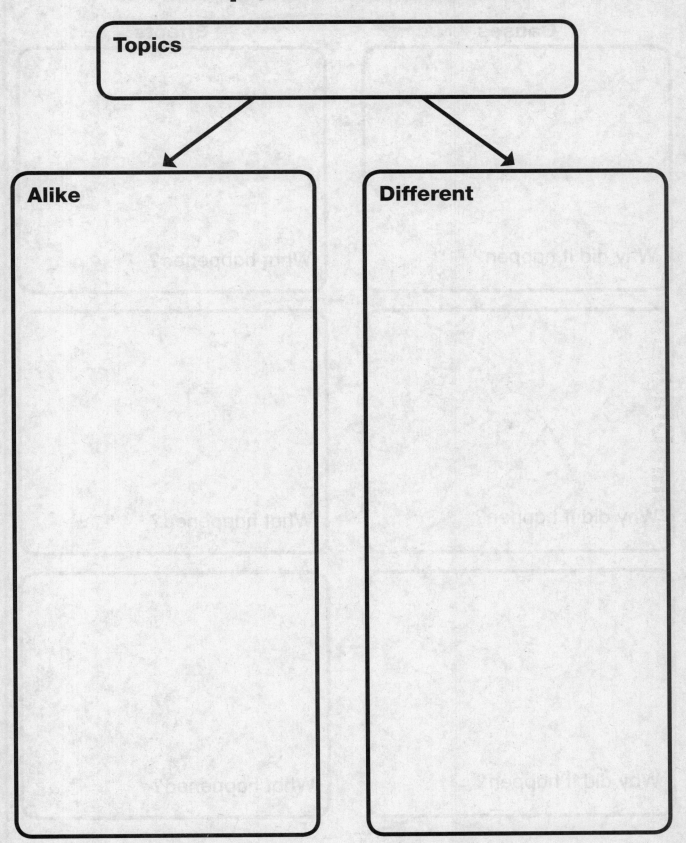

Topics

Alike

Different

Cause and Effect

Causes **Effects**

Why did it happen? What happened?

Why did it happen? What happened?

Why did it happen? What happened?

Problem and Solution

Problem

Attempts to Solve the Problem

Solution

Time Line

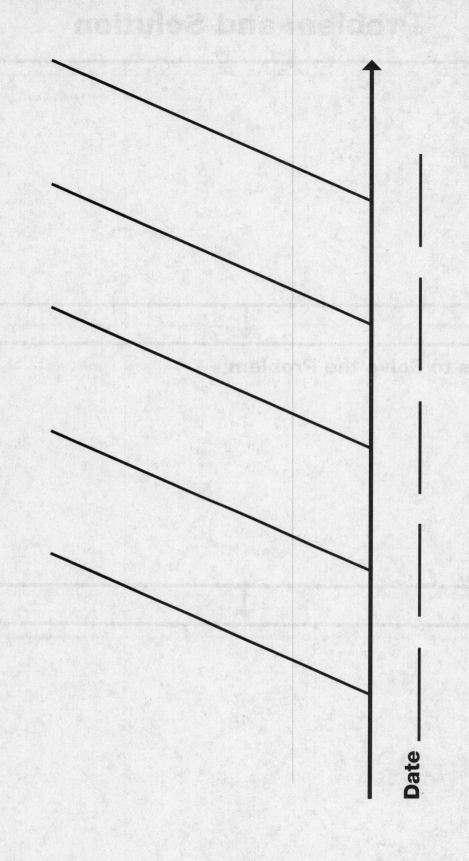

Date

Steps in a Process

Process _____

┌───┐
│ **Step 1**   │
│   │
│   │
│   │
└───┘
                      ↓
┌───┐
│ **Step 2**   │
│   │
│   │
│   │
└───┘
                      ↓
┌───┐
│ **Step 3**   │
│   │
│   │
│   │
└───┘

Three-Column Chart

Four-Column Chart

Four-Column Graph

Title _____

Answer Key

Leveled Reader Practice Pages

The California Gold Rush: A Letter Home p. 14

REALISM AND FANTASY

1.	R	4.	F	7.	F
2.	F	5.	R	8.	F
3.	R	6.	R		

The California Gold Rush: A Letter Home

p. 15 Vocabulary

1.	pick	4.	spell	7.	laundry
2.	mending	5.	skillet	8.	fetched
3.	boom	6.	coins		

9–11. Sentences will vary.

It's A Fair Swap! p. 18

SEQUENCE

1. People had no money, but they needed goods.
2. Native Americans bartered with Europeans for furs and skins and received things they couldn't make with their own tools, such as mirrors, beads, and shirts. Colonists traded with each other for what they needed.
3. As the country grew, people began to use money to buy goods from local merchants. Paper money was easier to handle and carry.
4. Money was used far more often than bartering. Bartering still survives today. Goods and services are traded on the Internet.

It's A Fair Swap! p. 19 Vocabulary

1.	carpenter	9.	carpenter
2.	knowledge	10.	thread
3.	marketplace	11.	straying
4.	plenty	12.	plenty
5.	straying	13.	merchant
6.	thread	14.	knowledge
7.	carpetmaker	15.	carpetmaker
8.	merchant	16.	marketplace

17–18. Sentences will vary.

Making Sense of Dollars and Cents p. 22

SEQUENCE

Possible responses given.

1–3. John met his friends outside. The friends walked to the mall. They all went to the bookstore.

4–6. John and his friends grabbed their favorite comic books. John realized he didn't have enough money to pay. John's friends helped him buy the comic book.

Making Sense of Dollars and Cents p. 23 Vocabulary

1.	e	5.	f
2.	c	6.	a
3.	g	7.	d
4.	b		

Paragraphs will vary but should demonstrate students' understanding of the meanings of the words and correct usage.

Davis Buys a Dog p. 26

REALISM AND FANTASY

1. Yes; Possible response: Davis walks home from school.
2. Yes; Possible response: Davis delivers newspapers on Saturdays.
3. Yes; Possible response: Davis thinks to himself, *I can do that!*
4. realistic story

Davis Buys a Dog p. 27 Vocabulary

Possible responses given for 1–5.

1. amount; how much there is of something
2. earn; to get something by working for it
3. check; a piece of paper used to get money from a bank
4. million; a thousand thousands
5. thousand; ten one hundreds
6. worth
7. expensive
8. amount
9. interest
10. value

E-Pals p. 30

CHARACTER AND SETTING

Possible responses given.

1. They like to write letters; they like each other; and they are friendly people.
2. They want to get to know each other better.
3. an exclamation point
4. Juma sends a gift; they are very interested in each other's lives; and they are excited about seeing each other in person.
5. Molly mentions the 4th of July on page 7.

E-Pals p. 31 Vocabulary

1. ARRANGED put in a specific order
2. WOBBLED moved unsteadily from side to side
3. ERRANDS short trips taken to do something
4. EXCITEDLY with high emotions
5. STEADY firm in position or place
6. DANGEROUSLY hazardously
7. BUNDLES groups of objects tied together
8. UNWRAPPED removed the outer covering of something
9. Sentences will vary.

Antarctica: The Frozen Continent p. 34

MAIN IDEA

Possible responses given.

1. Antarctica is very windy and dry.
2. Scientists call Antarctica a desert.
3. The small amount of snow that falls in Antarctica never melts.
4. Snow is moved around by the wind until it freezes into ice.

Antarctica: The Frozen Continent

p. 35 Vocabulary

1. d
2. e
3. f
4. c
5. a
6. g

7. b
8. frozen
9. flippers
10. pecks
11. hatch
Paragraphs will vary.

Sarah's Choice p. 38

CHARACTER

Possible responses given.
Sarah: didn't listen to her mother; didn't ask permission
Julia: just moved in; asked permission
Both: friendly; like blueberries

Sarah's Choice p. 39 Vocabulary

1. d
2. g
3. a
4. b
5. f
6. c
7. e

8. shocked
9. sadness
10. shivered
11. slammed
12. gardener
13. excitement
14. motioned

Metal Detector Detective p. 42

MAIN IDEA

Possible responses given.

1. Main Idea: There are rules you must follow before using a metal detector.
2. Detail: Metal detectors are not allowed on National Park Service lands.
3. Detail: Ask permission before you use a metal detector in public places.
4. Detail: If you are not sure whether you can use a metal detector, just ask.

Metal Detector Detective p. 43 Vocabulary

1. e
2. b
3. f
4. a
5. c
6. d

7. enormous
8. strain
9. scattered
10. shiny
11. collection

Growing Vegetables p. 46

AUTHOR'S PURPOSE

Possible responses given.

1. to show that when you don't water plants, they wilt
2. to tell about the different things you need to do to grow vegetables
3. to inform the reader how to grow a vegetable garden
4. They need water, weeding, and sunlight.
5. It's more fun for everyone, and the end result is better.

Growing Vegetables p. 47 Vocabulary

1. b
2. c
3. b
4. a
5. c
6. b
7. a

8. cheated
9. clever
10. bottom
11. crops
12. partners
13. lazy
14. wealth

Colonial New England p. 50

DRAW CONCLUSIONS

Possible responses given.

1. New England colonists had to make their own clothing. + Making your own clothing takes a lot of time and energy. → New England colonists had to work very hard to dress themselves.
2. Colonial girls wore long wool dresses and aprons. + Today most girls wear pants. → Colonial girls dressed very differently from girls of today.

Colonial New England p. 51 Vocabulary

1. spoil
2. peg
3. steep
4. barrels
5. cellar
6. clearing

Paragraphs will vary but should use four vocabulary words correctly in context.

Gardening with Grandpa p. 54

CAUSE AND EFFECT

1. i	6. a
2. c	7. e
3. d	8. b
4. g	9. f
5. j	10. h

Gardening with Grandpa p. 55 Vocabulary

1. sprouting	9. beauty
2. humor	10. showers
3. blooming	11. bulbs
4. recognizing	12. doze
5. showers	13. blooming
6. bulbs	14. humor
7. beauty	15. Recognizing
8. doze	

The Elk Hunters p. 58

AUTHOR'S PURPOSE

Possible responses given.

1. to show that people working together can accomplish great things; to entertain
2. They lived in what is now Washington state; they hunted elk.
3. to show that they honored the elk that they hunted
4. to make me laugh; to entertain
5. because no one spoke the same language

The Elk Hunters p. 59 Vocabulary

Sentences will vary for 2, 4, 6, 8.

1. a the horns on an animal's head
3. b to form a mental image
5. a the words people use to communicate
7. b to hear without the speaker's knowledge

Paws and Claws: Learn About Animal Tricks p. 62

DRAW CONCLUSIONS

1. Tracks make patterns.
2. Many animal tracks show four toes.
3. Fireflies and bees don't leave tracks.

Possible responses given.

4. Harry was sad.
5. Annie was afraid of dogs.

Paws and Claws: Learn About Animal Tricks p. 63 Vocabulary

1. notepad	5. flutter
2. flutter	6. patch
3. dew	7. Fireflies
4. budding	8. hawkmoth

9–11. Sentences will vary.

Rescuing Stranded Whales p. 66

GENERALIZE

Generalization: There are many things to do to help a stranded whale.

Possible responses given.

Detail #1: pour water and ice on beached whale

Detail #2: herd whales and push into deeper water

Detail #3: take whales to aquarium first for care

Rescuing Stranded Whales p. 67 Vocabulary

1. chip
2. bay
3. melody
4. channel
5. surrounded
6. anxiously
7. blizzard
8. supplies
9. symphony

Do Animals Have a Sixth Sense? p. 70

🔄 **COMPARE AND CONTRAST**

1. howl
2. dig
3. hide
4. leave their hive

Possible responses given.

5. Animals behave unusually before a natural disaster.
6. Some animals try to run away, other animals try to find a safe place, and still other animals make noise.

Do Animals Have a Sixth Sense?

p. 71 Vocabulary

1. f
2. g
3. h
4. i
5. e
6. a
7. b
8. c
9. d

10. earth + quake = earthquake
11. fire + works = fireworks

The Lessons of Icarus p. 74

🔄 **CAUSE AND EFFECT**

Possible responses given.

a. Daedalus was an inventor and a builder.
b. Theseus wanted to slay the Minotaur and marry the king's daughter.
c. King Minos knew that Daedalus had helped Theseus.
d. They planned to fly out of the prison and escape.
e. His son Icarus had drowned.

The Lessons of Icarus p. 75 Vocabulary

1. drifting
2. complained
3. giggle
4. swooping
5. glaring
6. attention
7. looping
8. struggled

Measuring the Weather p. 78

🔄 **COMPARE AND CONTRAST**

1. wind speed
2. miles per hour
3. rainfall
4. inches
5. they both measure changes in the air. a thermometer measures changes in air temperature and a barometer measures changes in air pressure.

Measuring the Weather p. 79 Vocabulary

1-b. the distance from the top to the bottom
2-d. to run faster than someone or something
3-e. the quality found by dividing the sum of all the quantities by the number of quantities
4-a. the pointed top of a mountain or hill
5-c. dry, sandy region without water or trees

Paragraphs will vary. Sentences should show correct usage of each vocabulary word listed above.

The Rock Kit p. 82

🔄 **GENERALIZE**

Granite is usually gray; Sandstone is soft and sandy; Limestone is often white.

The Rock Kit p. 83 Vocabulary

1. chores
2. label
3. attic
4. stamps
5. board
6. spare
7. customers

Responses will vary.

The English Channel p. 86

🔄 **FACT AND OPINION**

1. fact
2. fact
3. opinion
4. fact
5. opinion

7–10. Responses will vary.

The English Channel p. 87 Vocabulary

1. current
2. medal
3. continued
4. drowned
5. stirred
6. continued
7. drowned
8. stirred
9. strokes

Answers will vary. Paragraphs should describe an achievement and correctly use the word *celebrate*.

Buck's Way p. 90

PLOT AND THEME
Possible responses given.
1. He would not have realized what a fast swimmer he was.
2. asked an older duck to teach him to swim
3. Buck learned to swim like the other ducks.
4–5. Answers will vary.

Buck's Way p. 91 Vocabulary
Possible responses given.
1. held tightly
2. repeated, as a sound
3. a long, narrow ditch
4. tall plants that grow in ponds
5. rushed or struggled
6. area of land between mountains
7–10. Students' stories should reflect that they understand the meaning of four vocabulary words.

East Meets West p. 94

COMPARE AND CONTRAST
Similar: Japanese girls display dolls in their homes. Japanese students love comic books. Japanese students march to drums.
Different: Japanese dolls are dressed like royal people. Japanese students march to taiko drums. Japanese have special holidays for boys and for girls.

East Meets West p. 95 Vocabulary
Answers will vary.

The American Dream p. 98

PLOT AND THEME
1. Fact. It can be proved.
2. Opinion. A statement of belief, can't be proved
3. Fact. It can be proved.
4. Opinion. A statement of belief, can't be proved
5. Fact. It can be proved.
6. Fact. Some people came to the U.S. for a better education.
7. Fact. In the U.S., public schools promise free education for all.
8. Opinion. Maybe the schools there were not good.
9. Opinion. Maybe they could not afford the school.

10. Fact. They could not afford to send their children to school.

The American Dream p. 99 Vocabulary
1. mention
2. twist
3. popular
4. custom
5. public
6. overnight
7. famous
8. admire
Responses will vary.

A Child's Life in Korea p. 102

SEQUENCE
1. d
2. c
3. e
4. b
5. a

A Child's Life in Korea p. 103 Vocabulary
1. sick
2. well
3. drops
4. port
5. described
6. farewell
7. memories
8. Curious
9. delicious
10. homesick

The World of Bread! p. 106

DRAW CONCLUSIONS
Possible response: The dough is shaped in a circle and browned in a frying pan. + It is held over an open flame which causes the bread to puff up. → This bread has big air pockets in it.

The World of Bread! p. 107 Vocabulary
1. braided
2. mixture
3. knead
4. boils
5. ingredients
6. batch
7. bakery
8. dough
Responses will vary.

A Walk Around the City p. 110

AUTHOR'S PURPOSE
Possible answers are given.
1. to name different jobs in cities
2. to get me to take a walk around my city
3. to get me to think about what my city looks like
4. to show the different types of jobs in a city

A Walk Around the City p. 111 Vocabulary

1. pitcher
2. cardboard
3. feast
4. Fierce
5. treasure
6. ruined
7. flights

Responses will vary.

The Statue of Liberty p. 114

MAIN IDEA

1. b
2. b
3. b

Possible reponses given.

4. He loves to play frisbee on the lawn. He loves to roll on the grass. He naps under a tree.
5. You can get cavities if you don't brush. Your teeth won't be healthy. Your teeth won't look good.

The Statue of Liberty p. 115 Vocabulary

1. crown
2. liberty
3. torch
4. unforgettable
5. models
6. symbol
7. tablet
8. unveiled

Sentences will vary.

New York City's Chinatown p. 118

CAUSE AND EFFECT

Possible responses given.

1. Throughout Chinatown, you can hear people speaking Chinese.
2. Many Chinese traditions are maintained in Chinatown.
3. Some older residents of Chinatown are disappointed in the younger generation.
4. Some Chinatown residents practice Tai Chi.
5. Some people watch the celebrations from perches high above the city streets.

New York City's Chinatown p. 119 Vocabulary

1. foreign
2. perches
3. bows
4. foolish
5. recipe
6. narrow
7. chilly

Responses will vary.

A Different Drawing p. 122

FACT AND OPINION

1. F
2. O
3. O
4. F
5. O
6. F
7. O
8. F

9–10. Opinion; It is a statement of someone's judgment.

A Different Drawing p. 123 Vocabulary

1. expression
2. native
3. settled
4. encourages
5. social
6. local
7. support

Paragraphs will vary.

Leo and the School of Fish p. 126

PLOT AND THEME

Leo and the School of Fish; a fish named Leo; under the sea; Leo swims away from the school to look at a ship; Leo confronts a lantern fish; he confronts a moray eel; he gets caught in a net but is able to swim through it; he rejoins the school. It's best to stick with the group.

Leo and the School of Fish
p. 127 Vocabulary

1. journey
2. scoop
3. crystal
4. discovery
5. joyful
6. disappeared
7. goal
8. unaware

Responses will vary.

Glass Blowing p. 130

GENERALIZE

1. Need very hot furnace—2500°F
2. Need safety goggles and gloves
3. Cannot blow too gently
4. Cannot blow too hard
5. Glass breaks easily
6. Must be cooled slowly

Possible responses given.

7. Factories can easily make many identical glass objects.
8–10. Factories use machines; machines are controlled by computers; factories use molds.

Glass Blowing p. 131 Vocabulary

Possible responses given.

1. tune; The musician played a beautiful tune on her guitar.
2. bursts; When you blow too hard through the rod, the glass bubble bursts.
3. puff; You need to puff through a rod to make a bubble.
4. factory; Glass bottles are made in a factory.
5. burros; Burros were used to pull wagons.
6. reply; I will reply to your question when I finish this work.
7. glassblower; A glassblower wears safety goggles and gloves.